5P1R1T R3V3L4T10N5

...everyday spiritual guidance.

Nigel Peace

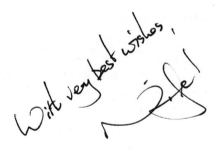

Local Legend Publishing UK

A Record of this Publication is available
from the British Library

ISBN 978-1-907203-14-5

Local Legend Publishing 2010
Park Issa
St Martin's Road
Gobowen, Shropshire
SY11 3NP, UK
www.local-legend.co.uk

Cover Design by Titanium Design
www.titaniumdesign.co.uk

**THE STORY OF A PERSONAL SPIRITUAL
JOURNEY, OF UNFOLDING AWARENESS AND
OF TRANSFORMATION.**

Contents

Appendices

Nigel Peace

Preface

This is a very personal story. Telling it is the only honest way to give an account of the extraordinary spiritual phenomena that I have experienced over many years of a journey to learn more about the nature of this life and our part in it. I hope you will not think it self-indulgent; indeed in many ways it has been painful to describe intimate details. Risky too - I fully expect to be ridiculed by many, not least because several of the events recounted are almost literally incredible. Well, have you ever heard of Divine Guidance by car registration plates…?

The trouble is this: there are many New Age writings which purport to teach us about aspects of 'the spiritual path'. Some are very thoughtful and genuinely helpful; many more are just ephemeral or bald statements of 'channelled Truth' which can insult the intelligence. (By the way, you should know right away that this book will *not* tell you The Secret of Life, let alone The Truth About Everything, because I don't know it; I dare say that there may well be some inescapable conclusions to be drawn from my experiences, but so far I have managed to escape most of them.) Most of these writings, good or bad, tell us that there is much 'guidance' to be had along our way, from the spirit worlds or from signs and omens, if we only knew "how to listen and look".

But very few of the writings ever actually describe this 'guidance' or give down-to-earth examples of it that the rest of us can understand or evaluate.

So how is anyone to learn how to recognise it? How are we to know which state of mind to cultivate? Most importantly, supposing we have got as far as to receive some guidance (perhaps, for example, simply through recalling an important dream), how are we to learn how to interpret it – sort the wheat from the chaff, the vision from the desire – unless we share these experiences with each other, discuss different ways of analysing them, and profit from each other's mistakes? Maybe only then can we begin to learn what it really means to be human…

7

Nigel Peace

So this is an honest and verifiable account of the phenomenal guidance that I have experienced on an almost daily basis during a particular period of about ten years. I believe that everyone can experience and learn from similar events. My story also includes many mistakes and foolish misinterpretations. I hope that others may learn from these.

Please try to read this story with an open mind or at least an open heart, and focus not so much on the ragged course of my life (though I'm sure many will recognise the same personal troubles that I have known) as on the mysterious events that accompany and sometimes illuminate it. That's why I've taken the risk of writing this.

After all, what does it mean 'to live spiritually'? For me, it is trying to live ethically, trying to be honest, to care for others and try not to cause hurt, to make one's life meaningful and experience it as fully as possible, to grow in understanding, to become all that we are capable of being – and to recognise the inevitability of messing up in all of these things! But, surely, we are *human* insofar as we can hold our hands up, try to make good and try again – living with an open heart, being prepared *to take risks*.

I believe that the experiences described here have extraordinary implications for our understanding of the mind and of what it is to be a human being.

May you be blessed on your journey.

I. *Finding the Way*

I was bored. The regular Saturday Spiritualist meeting had not been very illuminating, and the gossip afterwards was certainly not very spiritual. I sat with my cup of tea in the front room of the little terraced house in Wolverhampton, wondering exactly how we were supposed to access 'altered states of consciousness' let alone develop psychic abilities. It wasn't happening for me - perhaps I was too critical, or too young. I was in my early twenties, the other half dozen people in the room considerably older. But something quite incredible was about to happen which dramatically changed my attitudes.

This evening, one member of the group had arrived wearing a neck brace and clearly in great discomfort. She was actually a hospital nurse, but none of her colleagues seemed to have been able to alleviate her pain. The higher states of consciousness had been left behind in the back parlour for another week, but I suddenly found myself experiencing a vivid mental picture of placing my hands on her head in a certain way, and I somehow knew that this would help her. I shook my head but it just wouldn't go away. Even so, I was far too shy to mention it to the others. For one thing, I was the rookie of the group with very little real experience of these things. More importantly, my personal confidence was pretty low since I'd often been subjected to considerable derision from my family – including this very evening as I left home - for my interest in psychic things. But the vision was so insistent that eventually I told the others about it, suggesting that one or two of them who were known as 'spiritual healers' might carry it out. They pointedly refused, saying that it was my vision so I had to do it! What did I have to lose, since nobody outside those four walls would ever know about it? So I did what I had 'seen', feeling a powerful and peaceful energy flowing through me. Within seconds the lady became very quiet (which was a bonus, since normally she never stopped chattering) and ten minutes later the injury appeared to be cured; she said that the pain had gone, she took off the brace and never wore it again. This was my first experience of healing.

But something far stranger was yet to come.

As I drove home, still feeling quite stunned, I realised that I'd been following the same car for several miles and I noticed its registration number: LUK 853 E. I don't know why but somehow I read this as a Bible reference: the Gospel of Luke, chapter eight, verse fifty-three, and I felt compelled to look it up when I got home. The passage describes the healing of Jairus' daughter, whom everyone had believed to be beyond hope; the onlooking crowd had even laughed scornfully at Jesus.

The synchronicity of these events seemed to suggest that the car number had been a genuine 'omen' encouraging me in my spiritual search. And there was more…

One year later almost exactly the same situation happened again. In the same Spiritualist group, out of nowhere I began to feel a strong sense of premonition (butterflies in the stomach) and shortly afterwards a neighbour called in unexpectedly, asking for healing. I was persuaded to help and again my 'efforts' seemed to be successful.

On the way home later I found myself following a car with registration LUK 946 E which I read as Luke, chapter nine, verses four to six: Jesus commissions his disciples to go out preaching and healing.

I told no-one about these experiences – I was shocked and very self-conscious about it all.

But then the very next day the speaker at the Spiritualist church service I attended chose *exactly the same text* for her reading.

This was particularly remarkable because Spiritualist speakers are free to choose any reading whatsoever, or none, for their theme and indeed they very rarely choose one from the Bible anyway.

What on earth was going on? Was this Divine Guidance? Or meaningless coincidence? Or was I in fact, er, mad?

Φ

As a teacher of mathematics and statistics, I suggest that we should all be well aware of the unimportance of coincidence!

Perhaps we go to a football match and find that each team has a player with the same name, who both score a goal and both later get sent off. Maybe a woman goes to a party and sees another woman wearing an identical dress, and it turns out that they come from the same home town and their husbands do the same job. There are also some famous examples, such as Abraham Lincoln becoming US President in 1860 then being assassinated in the Ford Theatre, while John Kennedy became President in 1960 and was assassinated in a Ford Lincoln car, and so on. These are interesting events to talk about, but they are hardly enlightening and do little for our understanding of life. Coincidence just happens sometimes.

But then there is synchronicity. The sort of events I experienced are literally shocking. Their probability is unimaginable, and they held a *personal meaningfulness* that directly affected the future course of my life.

Well, I simply do not know if there is actually any purpose to our lives. Personally I just want my life here and now to be as worthwhile as possible because if nothing else this is a way to be at peace. But something very strange and disturbing had entered my experience, and how was I to deal with it?

There is nowadays a plethora of well intentioned gurus prepared to tell us 'the true meaning of life' and 'the nature of the soul' (and thus, by implication, how we should live); some of this information has even, apparently, come from 'Ascended Masters Of Wisdom'. There are mediums and near-death experiences and past-life recollections and so on, not to mention ancient mystical teachings. Hmmm, but is there any real *evidence*?

Well, we should not just dismiss all these things, surely, for many of the accounts are undoubtedly honest, often humbling and frequently mind-boggling. We certainly don't know everything there is to know about the nature of life. Our knowledge and understanding move on, sometimes hesitantly and sometimes in leaps of inspiration, and yet there is always more… We can see a few thousand stars with the naked eye. With a decent telescope it's millions. With a deep space telescope, many billions. Yet there is even further to go. We do not understand much about energy and even less about consciousness, for example, and these are fundamental to knowing what a human being is. There are so many phenomena which undoubtedly happen but which we cannot explain, and it will probably always be so. Therefore a certain open-mindedness and humility are a Good Thing.

Equally, however, it is downright silly if not also dangerous to keep a mind so open that it is prepared to swallow whole almost any fashionable, comforting or appealing belief that the latest guru offers, invariably without a shred of down to earth evidence or a critical examination of alternative explanations. Such gullibility robs us of perhaps the most important characteristic of a decent human life, our personal responsibility. We have to make our own minds up, experience life with thoughtfulness and a sense of purpose; yes, of course we must also listen to our teachers (and *anyone* at any moment can be our teacher), but without suspending our reason. We must be ruthless in distinguishing between what we *want* to be true and what *is*.

We wouldn't buy a television from someone without knowing that it worked. Even less, then, should we buy into a spiritual philosophy without evidence at some level that it at least helps us to live better lives. [1] On the other hand, we don't have to know *how* the TV works before we buy it.

---

[1] Take the case of survival of death. There can be very few of us who do not desperately long for the knowledge that we shall continue as individual personalities beyond this life, that there are angels and guides to support us, even that we might get another chance on Earth later... This would be the most incredibly comforting knowledge with immense implications for how we live now. And there are some extraordinary mediums who seem to offer evidence of survival (although for every one of these there are a hundred appalling ones plying their vague and mindless trade among the hopeful and broken-hearted).

But what is the quality of even the 'good evidence' that some mediums offer: are there clear and verifiable names, addresses, dates and factual accounts of events which could not possibly be known otherwise? And even when we strip down the accounts to those very few which do seem highly evidential, shouldn't we then consider alternative explanations such as clairvoyance, telepathy or the collective unconscious (for extraordinary as these are in themselves, they don't have the same implications for the nature of the human soul)? Moreover, there are very few of these wonderful accounts compared with the billions and billions of human

Perhaps I was just seeing significance where there was none? Human beings often look for connections in random phenomena (apophenia), or see meaningful images where there are none, such as faces in the clouds (pareidolia).

These are examples of what statisticians call a Type I error, the belief that something significant has occurred when the event is actually by chance. If a fire alarm system fails under test and we replace it because we think it's faulty, when in fact only a fuse had blown, this is a Type I error and we have lost some money. The opposite tendency to believe that nothing significant has occurred, when actually it has, is called a Type II error. If we don't replace the system because we think that probably there was just a blown fuse, when actually there was a serious fault, this is a Type II error and we may lose some lives.

One major problem with this is that the very idea of randomness is alien to us - seeking patterns and meaning is a very sensible thing to do, not least for our survival. If we are walking down a dark lane and mistake a shadow ahead for an attacker, at least we are prepared; Type I errors can be preferable to Type II!

Moreover, finding patterns and meanings can lead to creative leaps in our thinking, and we need such creativity in order to discover the underlying 'laws' of the universe that are hidden behind apparent chaos. Science is itself a deliberate and rational search for order, but that does not mean it always has to be 'logical'; its history is full of discoveries made, despite a lack of hard evidence, through creative and intuitive thought, or by sheer accident, and even through dreams (for example, the DNA double helix, the atomic structure of benzene, penicillin, continental drift...).

My experiences were surely more than just coincidence. To deny them entirely could be a Type II error. But to decide if they had any real meaning would require a healthy balance between scepticism and humility, between the need for evidence and the need

---

deaths there have been and therefore the billions and billions of souls who presumably would have wanted to communicate with their loved ones left behind and yet have not managed it... Clearly, even if there is a 'spirit world' then communication with it is extremely difficult and highly suspect!

to admit how little we know. And in any case, there are many *different ways of knowing*, just as the artist experiences life very differently to the engineer. The key must be whether our experience seems to work for us, to be important for us, in becoming better human beings. In other words, is there any point to it?!

As you might imagine, from the time of my Bible signs I started deliberately noting what seemed to be significant omens: not just car registrations but also important coincidences such as perhaps hearing a particular song at an appropriate moment or seeing an apposite slogan or name just as I was thinking of some relevant issue… Of course, one could get quite neurotic about this sort of thing: not *every* car number, song or slogan can contain a 'message'. I certainly found that it is all too easy to become obsessive about such experiences, especially when life is troublesome and one needs some tlc. One also needs some self-discipline (although, on the other hand, total scepticism must logically block one's awareness of such events! Nothing can be seen with eyes closed). I decided that only those omens that occurred at special moments or in especially strange circumstances may prove of value. Even so, for a long time, these events didn't make a lot of difference in my life. Until later, when they became much more frequent, regular and powerful. At that point, they started to turn into some kind of 'evidence'…That is one reason for this book being written.

Another reason is to try to show that, by our approach to these things, we can actually change our behaviour and grow spiritually.

Φ

So now I'd better put my cards on the table. This is a love story. What I mean is not that it is an account of my love for one particular woman, but of my learning about human love through several relationships. There are those who believe that we come to this life with a pre-ordained or even perhaps personally planned purpose, a set of lessons which our soul needs to experience in order to approach 'enlightenment'. Earthly life is a huge school where we undergo one course after another, one examination after another, until we have exhausted either our bodies or our capacity to learn. Whatever the truth of this, surely we all recognise if we are honest with ourselves that there are definite things we should try to learn if we want to be more at peace with ourselves and others. This, then, *is* our purpose. I believe that mine is to learn about love.

As a school teacher, I have often invited students to suggest alternative approaches to dealing with a new mathematical problem which they have encountered. The first suggestion is invariably to ignore it and do something else! Many of us do just that quite successfully for long periods in our lives even when we recognise that there is a problem to deal with. But fortunately both life and the mathematics syllabus have a way of presenting us with this same issue again sooner or later. Suppose, then, that we have decided to address it. A sensible idea is to try and relate it to similar problems we have encountered before and to adopt familiar methods. There can be two snags here, the first being that we must have sound knowledge of the facts and methods that we came across earlier. Students of life, no less than students of school mathematics, are notorious for failing to learn as we go along, for making the same mistakes we made before and having to retake our tests.

But even the most conscientious student who has revised continuously and practised thoroughly will inevitably meet the second and crucial snag: sometimes the problem facing us will require knowledge or methods that we simply haven't come across before, and we have to start over with learning something entirely new. This can be incredibly daunting. I have the utmost admiration for those who enter upon such unfamiliar territory with excitement and curious anticipation; it demonstrates a rare strength of character to walk into the unknown and risk failure, knowing that much of one's previous learning will be useless. Sooner or later, this challenge comes to us all.

But I am getting ahead of myself. The first and perhaps most difficult step of all is to identify the problem! I realised quite early in my life that the greatest challenges for me were about security – partly material (anxiety about money and home comfort) but mostly emotional (a need for loyal and loving relationships). I'm sure it's just the same for very many other people. But we all have our own individual circumstances, our unique genes and environment, which determine our challenges and our individual ways of meeting (or avoiding) them.

I was particularly sensitive to emotional pain, to rejection and the abuse of trust, and especially in relationships with women. I never managed to develop a 'thick skin', nor the sunny philosophical disposition I so admired in others who seemed able to take emotional knocks in their stride. The pain of several pretty extreme experiences was felt deeply. Does any of this sound familiar?

Oddly enough, I didn't become mistrustful but managed to develop an attitude to life that actively sought out new challenges and experiences, for example by changing my career path and by travelling. I became self-reliant and was seen as outwardly confident. I knew 'how things should be done' and I organised things excellently. People thought I was competent and strong. But what had happened, of course, was that inner defensive walls had been built, and limits set as to how much I was able to give and to receive.

This is a huge weakness, a strategy for avoiding the problem! Gradually I realised that I was failing. I was growing and learning, but only in my head. The inner barriers were being pushed back but rarely broken down, and if one set of walls fell over, others were being hastily erected. When my marriage failed in 1995, I knew I had hit the student's crucial snag: I had to learn an entirely new way of being.

But how is that possible?

Leaving aside the idea of 'fate', many of us certainly recognise that there are rhythms and patterns in our experiences. The same challenges keep coming up. We keep responding in the same way to certain situations. The more mindful we are of these, hopefully the better we are able to do things the next time. This is being the 'conscientious student', learning as we go along. For example, it may simply be a matter of realising that "I am behaving just like my father did..." But maybe these patterns are so deep that we can do nothing about them? Should we not just 'accept ourselves for what we are' (and insist that others do the same)?

This is giving up! It is perfectly clear that however entrenched a pattern may be, we *can* still make different choices however hard that may be. You can choose, for example, *not* to react like your parents did. You can choose *not* to accept an opportunity that has opened up to you, however valuable or exciting it may seem, because you may not feel ready for it or you just feel comfortable as you are. You may be lucky enough to get two different but exciting job offers at the same time. These are all real choices. So because to all intents and purposes we do seem to have free will, *then we do*. We are not determined by fate.

Yes, there may be some pretty powerful forces pushing us in certain directions and there will be times when resistance is downright foolish. Think of it as travelling along a river. There are times when we simply have to go with the flow, mindful of the current and the rocks and the weirs but with little control; yet there will be other times of relative calm and there will be tributaries that we can choose between – we might even be able to divert the flow entirely! Wisdom is about knowing the river. I decided that I had to start learning all over again, and let the river teach me.

I had to try to give up control and accept that I didn't know where to go.

This meant inviting 'higher guidance' and taking my strange experiences more seriously. Being a mathematician and naturally analytical, however, of course I couldn't stop trying to *understand* what was going on. But this had to be balanced with other non-rational ways of knowing and accepting that there may be subtle, paranormal energies at work in our lives. The first step was how to put this new attitude into everyday practice...

It seemed important to try to live quietly, the better able to hear, and as far as possible in harmony with nature. It would also be valuable to adopt a regular spiritual practice, a daily period of quiet inner vision. There would have to be a willingness to experience life as fully as possible, on as many levels of consciousness as possible, *to follow wherever the river led* whatever the pain and discomfort. Education is about personal change and that is never easy. Without wishing to stretch the school analogy too far, and in case all of this sounds horribly serious and gloomy, I want to say right now that:
- yes, life can be a serious and sometimes painful business, and if you want to learn about it the tests do keep coming one after

another and getting harder (like GCSE, then HND or AS and A2 Levels, then university degree, and then it *really* starts);

- but the rewards are literally wonderful too, from realising how very strange, powerful and clever the human mind is to feeling the magical beauty of spiritual experience and connecting deeply with other people. School students often seem to think that life cannot be worth living after about thirty years of age... I have news: the most joyful experiences of my life came in my late forties and beyond.

Φ

And so I made the deliberate decision to keep a careful record of my journey, and try to understand the path. There were three kinds of personal paranormal experiences that I learned from: readings of the I Ching oracle, my dreams, and of course the sort of signs and omens I described earlier. Many of these will be described in this account and labelled IC, D, and S.

Here are some examples showing why I think these things to be so important.

THE I CHING

The Book of Changes is of ancient Chinese origin; originally mainly a set of oracles, it developed into its present form of ethical guidance about three thousand years ago. Its central theme is that all life undergoes continuous change and transformation according to natural rhythms and cycles. If we can understand these, it helps us to make wiser choices in life.

When we consult the book about some vexing question, we are directed to one of sixty-four 'hexagrams' (six-line patterns). Each one has a general commentary describing the significance in human circumstances of a certain kind of situation. (More information about how to use the book is given in Appendix A.) Nobody knows quite how it could be that this description invariably closely matches the question posed; presumably it is some kind of psychokinesis. The reading will usually draw our attention to specific lines of the pattern, and associated with each of these is a more detailed description of the forces at work in our individual circumstances. These are the factors undergoing change or movement and the reading will offer some ethical advice here as to how to deal with the issue. It is always assumed, though, that we have entirely free will in understanding and responding to this. The final step in the consultation is to look at the new hexagram that will result when these 'moving lines' have eventually changed their nature; this resulting reading then describes the likely outcome if we heed (or do not heed!) the advice.

So, yes, the I Ching *is* a form of oracle but it is *not* an instrument of 'fortune telling' - its purpose is to help us understand the true nature of the situations we find ourselves in so that we can develop a spiritual attitude in our approach to them. The fact that this book is still in continuous and widespread use (the oldest book in continuous publication in history) is testimony to the accuracy and helpfulness that countless people ascribe to it, even if we haven't the faintest idea how it works…

I was very fortunate to be introduced to it in September 1982, through a mutual friend, by a serious China scholar who taught me its underlying philosophy. He also taught me, in no uncertain terms, the serious attitude of mind required for its use! This is not a simple tool of prediction. It demands a mindful and indeed reverent attitude towards the important developments in our lives. If we consult it on frivolous matters, the response will be dismissive! Its language and symbolism are not easy to understand (although at times its words are just astonishingly clear and apposite). Therefore there have been several translations in recent years that offer alternative interpretations with varying levels of sophistication, some very down-to-earth and simplistic. I have tried some of these but always go back to what many others agree is the truest rendering of the spirit of the original, by Richard Wilhelm. I approach each reading as if it were a meeting with a spiritual guide, calming my mind, focusing on my question, preparing the room to shut out the distractions of the everyday world and approaching the event with a prayer for 'higher' guidance.

A few weeks after my introduction to the book came my first proper opportunity to use it. I had been considering a new teaching job, a promotion with more money. It seemed like a good career move and I was offered the job after an interview, but before making my final decision I wanted to consult the book.

IC	**3rd November 1982: "Will my change of job be successful?"**
— x —	**This refers to Hexagram 62: "Preponderance of**
— —	**the Small."**
— o —	**The Judgement, or general commentary,**
— o —	**describes a situation of struggle and of**
— —	**achievement in small things only, with a need for**
— x —	**a conscientious and modest attitude.**
	Not very auspicious!

It is fairly unusual to find four 'moving lines' (suggesting much change) in a reading. Counting from the bottom, the first is a 'moving yin' line, the third and fourth are 'moving yang' lines and there is another 'moving yin' at the top. Looking at the interpretations of these, there were references to "misfortune", a danger of "attack or injury", a need for "great determination" and the likelihood of "disaster if one presses on too forcefully or too far".

This was all pretty unequivocal. Yet the book was *not*, as it were, telling me that I should not take the job – for we always have a choice – rather, that the experience was likely to be tough. When one proceeds with the reading and allows the moving lines to change (so the first and top lines becomes 'yang' while the third and fourth become 'yin'), a new hexagram results which represents the likely outcome of the situation. Here, it is Hexagram 27: "Nourishment". This describes personal and spiritual growth resulting from the experience.

So what should I do? I had felt optimistic about this opportunity, really wanted to leave my present post where I was frustrated, badly needed the extra money and had no 'evidence' to support the I Ching's verdict. And after all this was my first reading so I might have got it wrong anyway... I delayed my decision and two days later asked a further but rather different question.

IC   5th November 1982: "Is it God's will that I should go ahead with the new job?" (Meaning, would this be the right course from a spiritual point of view?)

This time the answer was Hexagram 35: "Progress", with the second and top lines moving. The interpretation of this was much more encouraging, describing "reward and advance" for one who "adopts a right and modest attitude despite sorrows". Further, "deserved happiness" would be received through the assistance of "a woman in authority"; and provided that one remained "determined but not forceful" the result would be Hexagram 40: "Release". So I was still being promised a hard time but, if I could deal with it properly, it would be rewarding.

I accepted the challenge and found myself embarked upon twenty months of torment and stress! It turned out to be an appalling school and I was given the lowest achieving and most ill-disciplined classes, with virtually no support from a weak management. There was indeed "misfortune" in the form of personal abuse, theft and vandalism of my property, and there was even "attack" in the form of an assault on me by a pupil. There were times when I almost did "go too far and too forcefully" in my determination to uphold my values… But I held on and just about kept control; moreover, *I really learned how to teach* and I certainly learned a lot about people. My character was strengthened, my understanding of the world advanced. I also wrote two books of mathematics material for my disaffected pupils (since the school had virtually no text books) and these were accepted for publication by the first company I approached, whose commissioning editor turned out indeed to be a woman. This gave me great satisfaction and happiness especially in such difficult circumstances. Then finally I seized an opportunity to change jobs again and was 'released' to an excellent school where I stayed for more than twenty-five years.

So the I Ching proved astoundingly accurate in this instance, a book written thousands of years ago even identifying literal events that I would experience as well as interpreting their personal meaning for my development. It doesn't always work so well. Sometimes the book's answers, while clearly apposite, are extremely difficult to understand or seem too vague to be useful. Maybe this is due to the reader's 'wrong state of mind', to poor preparation or to there being too much inner confusion or anxiety. I don't think anybody knows how it works or why it sometimes doesn't. Carl Jung, who wrote the introduction for the Wilhelm translation, said that given another lifetime he would devote the whole of it to studying the I Ching!

It seems to be, rather like dreams perhaps, a means of reaching into an inner stream of consciousness and reading its patterns (like dipping a hand into the river and feeling the current). Sometimes the waters are pure and clear, sometimes muddy. It shows us that the future is not determined, but that there may be more or less strong probabilities in how it will turn out; these outcomes depend upon our choices and, significantly, our attitudes. The book is certainly hot on attitude, much of its ethical advice being in the form of how 'the superior man' should respond to the situations it describes. Naturally, none of us can claim to be him, for however high our ideals we fall short of them time and time again. But the determined soul who keeps trying will find a wonderful personal relationship developing with this extraordinary book, almost as if indeed it is the voice of a wise and spiritual master. One just *knows* when the answer is clear and trustworthy. And if the message isn't clear, that's far more likely to be due to our poor understanding than to a deficiency of wisdom in our teacher.

DREAMS

In 1994 my school had two minibuses, one older but in better condition than the other, and I learned that they were to be sold off at a nominal price to make way for new ones. I made the Bursar a token offer of £100 for the older bus, intending to convert it into a campervan for holidays; the offer was accepted and we shook hands on the deal. On the 10th of April I did an I Ching reading about my project: the result described "**distrustful people**" and "**difficulties**" leading to "**grief**" and "**shock**". I was getting a warning but I really couldn't understand or believe it; so I tried again but the new reading also described "**others interfering with one's**

good intentions" and the matter being closed in **"a period of seven"**.

D   That same night I dreamed that I was returning home from abroad in a hired car. Near a crossroads I saw someone selling horses, a mare and a foal. I switched the hazard lights on and stopped to talk to the man, offering to buy the mare for £450. Still, I didn't feel sure about the deal. While I was deciding, I saw the police take my car away so I left to try and retrieve it without making the purchase. The dream ended with the police returning my car to me.

My interpretation ran like this: being abroad and hiring a car suggested a holiday time, while the crossroads and the hazard lights clearly indicated a decision to be made and perhaps danger; selling horses (that is, 'horse trading') is a cultural symbol of dishonesty; my car being taken away obviously meant that my progress or plans would be damaged, though without too much harm done since the car was later returned. I didn't know what to make of the other details and, perhaps stupidly, I didn't even connect the dream to the I Ching reading immediately – well, I trusted the Bursar and had no *reason* to believe anything was amiss in that situation.

Almost exactly seven weeks later on the 26th of May, the Bursar reneged on his promise, claimed that we'd never even discussed the idea let alone shaken hands on it, and put the minibus up for secret auction (I have never found out why). It was eventually sold to a colleague of mine – I had thought he was a friend and had discussed my plans with him – for £450. It now became clear that the two horses in the dream represented the minibuses (one older than the other) and it may be worth recording that the Bursar's name was clearly hinted at in the dream!

What is so remarkable about this dream is that it is not some vague premonition that something might go wrong with the deal, as if perhaps I'd picked up the man's body language and had had inner doubts.

No, this was an actual precognition of factual details, which nobody knew at that time.

Nigel Peace

Although there has been much excellent research and many interesting theories put forward, still nobody fully understands much about dreams, even about why we have them let alone what they mean. I started to become fascinated by mine as a child and gradually taught myself to be able to remember and record many of them. Typically I will wake up immediately after what seems to be a 'significant' dream and use a small tape recorder kept at the side of my bed to keep an account of it, which I will write up and study the next day. Over the years, my dreaming has become more and more often lucid, that is to say I am aware of dreaming while it is going on rather like watching a film (although, curiously, I am aware of being a character in the film at the same time). Therefore I am also able to study and begin to interpret the dream while it progresses. One can develop an attitude of detachment towards one's own mental events, just as for example we may be totally involved in playing a game and yet at the same time know that it is a game.

So while I cannot claim to be an expert on dreams, I can offer a few observations from my fifty years or so study of them... There are clearly several types. Some are pretty chaotic and involve recent events and impressions perhaps from the previous day or something we have seen on television; it is as if the brain is scanning all the information to decide what is important and worth remembering. I call these **Filing Dreams**. Other dreams seem to recall old memories, perhaps integrating past experiences with more recent events, or checking through old files to assess their continued usefulness so that they can then be discarded or stored in the attic to make room in our consciousness for new learning. These could be called **Spring Cleaning Dreams**. We all do exactly these sorts of things in our everyday lives with the masses of correspondence and bills and information leaflets, brochures and magazines that come our way.

But then there is another kind of dream which is more coherent, often developing some kind of episodic story and usually riddled with strange or archetypal symbolism; irrational things may be happening, the scenes and characters may change suddenly, yet the whole experience hangs together in a way that insists we take notice. Such a dream can seem to be quite long and can have a powerful effect on us. It seems as if the unconscious mind is trying to bring to our attention some important information which we cannot - or will not - grasp by normal conscious thought. Maybe it is something that we ought to know but have failed to recognise in our daily lives because of lack of evidence or maybe because we're afraid of what it means and the consequences it might have.

This kind of dream can be one of (at least) two kinds. The first arises from our deep-rooted anxieties or desires that have been suppressed – a **Therapy Dream**. The other is a dip into the stream of consciousness in order to make some sense of the underlying patterns in our lives (getting to know the river) – this might be a **Clairvoyant Dream**. It can be extremely difficult to distinguish between these two and, in any case, in my experience any one dream may be a mixture of all the above! [2]

---

[2] For example, if a dream seems to suggest that a significant event may occur in the future, is this actually what is going to happen, or may happen, or just what I want to happen? And if it is difficult to know what *type* of dream one has experienced, it can be even more of a challenge to understand its meaning. There are many psychological approaches. Most people who have studied the field recognise that there are certain archetypal symbols ('running upstairs' represents an improvement, a 'flash of light' means the solution to a problem). I started by using a respected 'dictionary of symbolism' that helped me to become familiar with the general language of the unconscious mind. But then many symbols are entirely personal and will mean different things to different people: for many, a dream of being 'at school' may suggest there is something important to be learned, whereas for a teacher, for whom school is an everyday experience, it could represent something entirely different. I have come to recognise that for me this symbol refers to my emotional relationships. However, there is an amusing snag here: once we think we have understood a certain symbol, in future our minds may seek out an entirely different symbol with which to convey similar information because, after all, it is trying to tell us something which we do *not* know rationally! So it is only through personal experience, study and self-awareness over a period of time that each of us gradually learns what our minds are telling us. Ultimately, although there may be common recognisable scenarios, we are the only ones who can really interpret the detail of our own dreams. Yet for all the difficulties this is surely one of the most fascinating of phenomena in human experience.

In case you are thinking that this is all too problematic, subjective or even pointless, I have to say that my dreams have often been unbelievably helpful to me in understanding how real life situations are developing on inner and as yet hidden levels. *Sometimes, as above, they actually foretell the future.*

But does the example I've given suggest that the future is in fact determined? Not at all. I have already said that we have plenty of experience of making real choices which lead to very different outcomes. Rather, my minibus dream seems to have been nothing less than time travel!

Occasionally, then, in dreams as with the I Ching, perhaps we can see the future with some clarity. But how can we tell when we have? It can only be a personal judgement based on our previous experience and on the coherence and impact of the dream or reading. And, yes, sometimes we're bound to make mistakes...

SIGNS

I described earlier my first experience of being guided by signs or omens. But what do these things really mean and where on earth do they come from? If they do have meaning, then they are some kind of 'psychic signposts' which indicate that one is on the right (or perhaps the wrong) path. For me, they are usually encouraging or reassuring, strengthening my resolve when life is hard. Sometimes they seem to warn me that my thinking about a particular matter is misguided. At other times they can even be predictive and are followed within a short time by some appropriate event.

If you haven't already stopped reading on the grounds that this account is plain ludicrous, I promise that you will simply not believe some of the signs that I will describe later... And there are moments when the circumstances, the meaningfulness and the sheer creativity of a certain synchronicity are so astonishing that *surely* it must have been deliberately and cleverly engineered by some intelligent force beyond me...

The existence of guiding spirits or 'guardian angels' sometimes seems the simplest and most obvious explanation. Yet it is one that I continue to resist despite my earlier interest in Spiritualism. Of course, like very many people I *want* to believe it; but as I have said earlier, there are too many profound implications, not to mention possible alternative explanations, even if some of those are equally outlandish. So I am *not* going to propose spirit worlds as The Truth. I prefer to think that our minds can somehow access an alternative or inner consciousness, where the underlying energies and patterns of our lives can be perceived more clearly than in the rush and noise of the everyday world. I therefore apologise publicly now to my spirit guides for denying and often ignoring them if indeed they are working so hard and so brilliantly to help me...

Many others have spoken or written about similar synchronous phenomena (although even Carl Jung seems to have missed car registration plates!) There is nothing special about my experience except perhaps that I have kept a careful record of hundreds of such instances. I am sure that *everyone* can develop awareness of this inner consciousness and see the signposts – everyone has experienced a really strange coincidence - just as everyone can record and study their dreams and everyone can read and learn to interpret the I Ching.

What I am going to describe now, everyone can experience. There are many ways of 'knowing'. All it takes is an open mind, an honest heart and a passionate desire to live a meaningful life.

II. *The New Path*

My second long-term relationship was hitting the rocks in ways frighteningly similar to the first. Situations were different of course, but I could recognise some patterns now. Sure, I had grown over the years and learned a lot, I was coping better than before with some of life's frustrations and challenges – but I was still hitting the barriers. I wasn't selfless enough to accept the things that were happening; it was making me ill and I just didn't know where to turn.

We tried psychotherapy but it didn't seem to be getting us anywhere and the pain was still intense. However, at the end of 1993 I experienced a period of what I can only call Grace, a kind of higher awareness of love that helped me somehow to transcend the problems, to believe there was light at the end of the tunnel…

Now, I'm not a great fan of astrology but Patrick Walker did often seem to have an unusual sensitivity and perception. In January 1994 his reading for my sign said:

S **"You are about to enter a period of change, excitement and adventure… encouraging you to seek new routes on to the path of greater enlightenment. However, nothing is ever gained without a certain amount of sacrifice… (It is) time to recognise that you are not chained to any destiny other than one of your own making."**

But if there is no fixed destiny, how could he suggest that my life was about to change? Perhaps this sort of 'forecast' reinforces what I had come to believe through more than ten years experience of the I Ching: there are patterns and rhythms in our lives, and times when we are presented with opportunities and challenges – but we always have a choice whether we accept these and how we approach them. One thing is pretty certain: change is often painful! Well, I chose to try the transcending route and asked my partner to marry me (we had lived together for nearly nine years).

IC   1ˢᵗ January 1994: "How will this year develop for me?"
Hexagram 54 is "The Marrying Maiden". The moving lines described one who is disappointed in love and lonely but staying loyal; marriage passes one by, but later one is rewarded. The eventual outcome is Hexagram 24: "Return (or, Turning Point)".

Like the previous example given of I Ching readings, this was not encouraging! But I chose to press on with my course and we married in March. Just five days later:

D   **22ⁿᵈ March, 1994. I am driving home on the A41, going too fast. I know there's going to be an accident – others will crash into me and I will be killed.**

That particular road has always been significant for me – I have lived near it many times and travel on it regularly, so it has come to represent 'the course of my life'. The dream was an unequivocal warning of danger and serious upsets ahead!

And by the end of the next month I had to recognise that the relationship had collapsed irretrievably. All the old problems had returned with a vengeance and my wife seemed disinterested in addressing them with me; there were family and financial crises, great stress in my career, and vandalism was just one of the signs of general chaos and breakdown of life... Car registration 'signs' referred to **betrayal**, there were dreams about **attack** and an I Ching reading spoke of "**Dissolution**" [3]. I felt emasculated, lonely and afraid; despite the ceremony, marriage was indeed 'passing by'. The light at the end of the tunnel was turning out to be a false dawn. Maybe it had been a glimpse of the future, of what could be, and after all the I Ching also described 'reward' and a 'turning point'. But right then everything was very dark and I was on my own.

My life became almost intolerably difficult now. I was trying to keep home and family and job together, but suffering severe stress illness that had me hospitalised more than once. The dreams

---

[3] You may be glad to know that I shall not list every sign, dream or reading in this account – there are thousands, but they *are* all documented.

kept coming. A particular theme recurred for more than nine months because I just wouldn't accept the truth of what it seemed to be telling me, that my wife would betray me. Eventually, as if in exasperation, my mind presented it so that the message was perfectly obvious.

D   22nd January 1995: I am at home in the lounge, on my knees with a severe wound in my abdomen caused by a knife attack. I am aware that elsewhere in the flat several people are painting the walls and doors white and I can feel their hostility as I stagger out to watch. There are three of them, people I know. All my decoration work is being whitewashed over, as if to wipe me out. Then in the kitchen I come face to face with another male teacher I know, sitting there calmly as if it is his home. I ask him what's happening and as he's about to tell me I wake up, feeling a powerful and painful energy.

Even now I couldn't really believe it (or didn't want to) and in fact it was almost exactly another year before it was publicly admitted that this man in the kitchen was indeed my wife's lover. (And a little later, he actually did move into that flat as his home!) Meanwhile, other dreams continued to warn me of forthcoming attacks, of separation, and of legal and financial problems.

Yet throughout all of this there had also been intimations of a happier future.

D   18th August 1994: I dreamed that I was the character Nigel in The Archers radio programme (one of my favourites), in a very good mood and talking to his fiancée. Then I had to go somewhere important, and crossed the road at a major junction; it was foggy and I was being very cautious, waiting for the lights to change. I crossed safely and continued north, arriving at an airport. There were two groups of four people there and someone was collecting our passports. All was well.

I have to admit that at the time I was still immersed in personal confusion, and the dream made little sense at all except for being vaguely optimistic. It probably meant something for my future because the character had my name. What was at least clear was that things would become difficult (fog) and I was going to have to make a major decision (the junction); I would have to be very careful and wait for 'the right time' (the lights). But I was also reassured that I was on the right path, because I 'crossed over' and went north (which is an archetypal symbol for 'the right direction'); this would lead to a new and happier journey (the airport, having a passport) when perhaps life would 'take off'...

Yet what is so extraordinary is the detail which I didn't - and couldn't − understand then. I do know that numbers in my dreams usually represent time periods, and over the next few years a double four or an eight featured frequently. It would later turn out that four years and eight years from the decisive time of changing direction would be critical points (which, incidentally, illustrates how my dreams often see a long time into the future). Even less could I know that a relationship with a woman with the same name as an Archer's character would be the most important experience of the first four year period!

About two weeks later another dream filled in some details.

D   **30th August 1994: I was a prisoner but had been allowed out of jail on a sixty-mile cycle ride, so I went to visit the home where I spent much of my childhood. I met my parents there; it was my father's sixtieth birthday and he looked very frail. They begged me to stay with them but I said I must 'do the right thing' and go back. "Still," I said, "I'll be free in one year." This was repeated. I rode on into Uplands Avenue and along to the park where I waited to be collected. It was five to six.**

Yes, I felt like a prisoner in my marriage at that time and I wanted some sort of comfort (home, parents − though my father had at this time been dead for nearly two years). Perhaps I wanted an escape. But my mind was impressing on me here that I must act honourably, while somehow I also knew that there would be a release and improvement (Uplands). I had to recognise that there was a natural 'cycle' involved (a nice example of the amusing puns that often turn up in dream language). This seemed to be reinforced by the repeated number sixty which is a cycle of the clock too. The time of five to six suggests one twelfth of a clock cycle; my wife and I had recently passed the twelfth anniversary of our meeting. So this again indicated to me 'a one-year period'. Throughout, the number six seemed especially important.

In the event, some ten months later my marriage would finally end in separation. And almost exactly one year after this dream, in early September 1995, I would meet Eve. But moreover, five years or sixty months after that, and precisely six years after the dream, another even more significant relationship would start... I'm sure you are now beginning to realise why I have come to trust my dreams.

January 1995 was perhaps my lowest point.

IC   I read the I Ching for the year ahead and was hardly surprised to receive Hexagram 6: "Conflict", which speaks of danger and 'dispute over possessions'. Yet it also foretold a 'significant meeting' later and the resulting Hexagram was number 44, "Coming to Meet", echoing my airport dream.

This unhappy period came to a head, perversely, on my birthday that year and the decision to divorce was made the next day. The night before, I had had one of my strangest ever dreams, one that I hardly understood at all at the time but which in retrospect was showing me exactly where the decision would lead.

D   17th June 1995: I filled my car with petrol at a garage on the A41 at Apex Corner, paying with two £2 notes and one £1 note. The cashier gave me two pennies change, one of them bent, and also a lottery scratch card. He showed me what to do with it since I didn't know – you win if the panels reveal pictures of women, which mine did. They also revealed the numbers 34, 35, 36 and 5. The cashier became very excited and said that the ticket was worth a lot.

This was clearly telling me something about my personal progress (fuel for my car, the A41 again) and especially my emotional life (the women). And strangely, given my deep

33

unhappiness at the time, there seemed to be a promise of good fortune (winning the lottery), maybe even some kind of ultimate happiness (Apex). Now consider the numbers here: I had had two marriages, and in the course of establishing my new path in life there were going to be two transformative relationships and one lesser one. One of these would involve dishonesty (bent coin) – in fact, Eve left exactly thirty-four months later. The number five was suggested twice – I met Alice exactly five years after the dream. And Apex Corner was on the route between our two homes.

Now, I realise that I could be accused of interpretation by hindsight. But the facts I have described are *true*. And the correspondence between them, the dreams and the I Ching readings, is startling. The inescapable conclusion is that I was somehow reading a future that could not possibly have been known at the time – there was just no evidence of it and the people involved had not even been met. This last dream cannot have been simply wishful thinking, and nor can the awareness of the dream possibly have brought about the subsequent events.

Isn't it enormously comforting to realise that in our darkest hours we can still see new light ahead?
As the I Ching teaches, life is change.

Φ

I could just not have imagined the change that was going on all around me now. I had really wanted my relationship and family to work and believed in a new way for us; marriage had been a solemn and holy intention and I now felt wretched for breaking the vows. But equally there was nothing I could do about it anymore, as if I was being carried along on the river's torrents despite myself and it was all I could do to keep my head down and somehow trust that the flow was taking me where I needed to go – to places where I could learn what I had to learn. Was this really what I wanted? On the thirteenth anniversary of my first dream about my wife, before I had met her, I asked the book whether continuing the divorce action was the right thing to do.

IC   22nd July 1995: the response was the Hexagram "Darkening of the Light", a very descriptive name. It talked of struggling to create order in one's life but also of eventual 'victory' after some considerable time. Again the result was "Return (Turning Point)", just as it had been at the beginning of 1994 when I was making the decision to marry...

Now, it is commonly accepted wisdom that when one important relationship has just ended is exactly the wrong time to begin another. But there was absolutely nothing I could do about it. It was as if the universe was saying to me: "Right, that's one chapter of your life over with and you said you wanted to learn new stuff and grow spiritually, so here's your next lesson." I met Eve in September and it was simply a powerful attraction that couldn't be ignored, as if we already knew each other and had to be together. Apart from anything else, the relationship brought me much comfort and happiness during the terrible months ahead of legal battles, financial and emotional threats, while I also tried to set up a new home. I don't know how I would have coped without her support. As time passed, naturally I wondered whether we might have a future together although I was also quite disturbed about our circumstances – although estranged from her husband, she was still married. This ethical dilemma soon gave rise to an important dream, again showing me the road ahead.

D   16th November 1995: I had been invited to help coach a badminton class at a sports centre on a certain road, but the other coach with me was lazy and rude, ignoring me. I couldn't find the light switches, became angry, and left the class, walking home in the dark. But then I went to an office where I talked to a receptionist about buying a new car; she offered to take my old car and give me £2000 off. I felt there was something not quite genuine about this offer. The woman was tall and slim with long hair and a strong attraction developed between us. Later I moved into a new house and this woman arrived as I was unpacking boxes.

Now, Eve worked at a sports centre and lived on that particular road, so the dream was telling me something about her. And although I did in fact coach badminton I have come to recognise this symbol as representing 'decisions' in my dreams. I was indeed trying to decide what was right in this situation, and my mind was apparently warning me that she would turn away and leave me 'in darkness'. Maybe I already suspected this deep down? But of course what I couldn't possibly know was that in the year 2000 would begin a second important relationship ('exchanging my car for a new one!') – this would be Alice, who was indeed tall and slim and with long hair. Thus I would find 'a new home' for a while, although again there might be something not quite right about it.

The dream confirmed my feeling that the relationship with Eve wasn't 'right', or at least that she was not the partner I needed in the long term, however lovely she was. This was not the way to reach the light. I wrote all this down at the time – and promptly ignored it. Well, the attraction between us and my need for her comfort were simply too strong, and men can be very weak...

As if I needed telling, the Debbie Frank horoscope for me at the beginning of 1996 was straight to the point.

S   **A new era had begun for me last autumn, in which relationships would affect me "as never before". I would have "the opportunity to learn a new way of relating to others", and would become more influenced by my emotions.**

And how! This was after all what I had intuitively known I needed, but that hardly prepared me for what was to come – my rational and analytical mind was going to be torn apart and rebuilt over the next few years. I had glanced at this horoscope with a vague interest when it was published because it happened to be in the newspaper I was reading, but kept it because it contained several intriguing predictions for the year which seemed very relevant to my circumstances. One by one they proved astonishingly accurate and right on cue, in domestic, financial and health matters. I know enough about the theory of astrology to dismiss the normally superficial readings in newspapers, but sometimes a particular individual astrologer just seems somehow to be getting things right. We can only judge on our own evidence.

For me at least, this sort of reading and the way events were beginning to turn out were strong evidence that I had indeed made the right decisions in changing the pattern of my life. Shortly, another incredible and wonderful sign would confirm it. Many of the awful legal troubles began to end, in quite surprising circumstances, as Easter approached. Against the odds (even my solicitor had advised me against this course), I won the final appeal hearing in court on the 9th of April.

S **I returned to my car after the hearing in a state of shock, elation and exhaustion. It was all over at last. As I began to drive home, I turned on the tape machine intending to listen to a play recorded earlier from the radio. But somehow I must have made a mistake in the recording and the radio had been tuned to the wrong channel. Instead of a play, I found myself hearing the Byrds' song 'Turn, Turn, Turn': "to everything there is a season and a time for every purpose under Heaven".**

This was so humbling that tears began pouring down my face and I had to park the car until I recovered. Who, or what, had arranged that for me?

By the end of summer, life was much more peaceful in most respects. But my emotional state was far from steady. Undeniably, I loved Eve and when we were together we were very happy. But we weren't together very often, mainly because of her personal circumstances, which she seemed unable to change; I still felt uneasy about the ethical problem and now frustrated about the relationship too. Further dreams warned that she might turn away from me while the I Ching told me that "**little can be achieved**"; enigmatically, however, it also said that "**inner forces of Fate**" were at work and that I should be patient...

But I was in a hurry for security and, new to the path, I was spiritually immature. I understood neither the point of the lesson that life was offering me nor how much personal rebuilding was still necessary. So I ignored the advice and began to consider the possibility of other relationships. Yes, the I Ching did warn me against this but I ignored it again, refusing to believe in any sort of 'Fate'; surely we must make our own decisions? Hmm, yes, and our own mistakes. One or two fledgling relationships quickly came to nothing because my heart just wasn't in them. Then, as one did seem to be developing further, I suddenly realised too late that I was betraying Eve. It doesn't matter whether she was being 'fair' to me or not; she had her own path, her own lessons and her own way of facing up to them, and I should have accepted that. Instead, I hurt her and undermined whatever growing confidence in me and in the possibility of change she may have felt. I was deeply sorry, and it was a savage lesson for which I would pay dearly later.

Now I started to learn. One who has consciously embarked on a spiritual path has a fundamental responsibility to, well, try to be spiritual!
Absolute integrity in every way is a basic requirement.

Whatever the source of guidance is, it is wonderfully merciful. Not only did Eve forgive me, so that we might continue with our lessons, my dreams now reminded me of the overall picture.

D   6ᵗʰ August 1996: I was taking a school team to play in **Norwich and went on ahead, discovering that due to a double booking we had to change to a different stadium. Then I found myself with the school Headmaster discussing exam results. They were good; two of my pupils had had their papers remarked and their grades were improved from E to A.**

Now, Norwich represents something very special for me, although I had only been there once, on a day trip about five years before. Quite by chance, in a small side street there I had found an object of great personal significance. After I began to use the I Ching I had several dreams about searching for a 'ting', which is an ancient Chinese pot representing sacrifice and nourishment. It had begun to assume the proportions of a Holy Grail for me! But despite having several Chinese friends and searching the Chinese areas of

London I hadn't been able to find one before. So going to Norwich signifies the achievement of a spiritual purpose for me. The dream suggested that this would involve a change in my plans or direction (a different stadium) and that there would be a change. E (Eve) would give way to A. Remember, this was still some four years before meeting Alice. Then as if to make sure I got the message, another dream two days later went even further.

D   8th August 1996: I was taking my son for his first day at secondary school and collecting his uniform in an area of my home town Wolverhampton (by now I was living in London) called Ash. It cost £700 less staff discount of 10%. Then I had to follow a new road system, almost got stuck in a dead end, but finally found my way.

I assumed that my son here represented me making a new start at a 'higher level'; and if school represents relationships for me, then I was looking ahead to a 'second' important encounter. In the event, there was indeed another short relationship after Eve, but it didn't lead anywhere (a dead end). Two other details of the dream meant nothing to me then but were to prove *astonishingly precognitive*. First the numbers: 700 less 10% is 630 – Eve left me exactly 633 days after this dream. (Sorry, yes, analysing numbers is just something I do.) Secondly, Alice's initial is of course A, which was prominent in both dreams this week.

Meanwhile back in the real world, little changed over the next year or so. Career difficulties began to ease and I was giving a lot of attention to my son, our new home and especially the garden – this really became an important metaphor for my new life as I gradually transformed it from a mixture of bare patches and overgrown wilderness to a lovely place of shape, contour, colour and growth where I found great peace. There were still irritations there (ants nests!) and I couldn't do all that I wanted to because of lack of money, but I was learning that transformation takes time…

My relationship with Eve also continued much as before, a strange mixture of insecurity and joy, of disquiet as her situation didn't change yet happy bewilderment as I realised that *I was changing*. For all the difficulties, she is a lovely and warm spirit whose presence was starting to melt my inner barriers, whose *feeling* was overcoming my way of *thinking*. Life was teaching me to **accept the unreasonable, tolerate the unacceptable, and have patience with the irrational** (in which being a mathematician certainly helped) – *all because the most important experience in human life is love.* For the first time, and on a daily basis, I was living from the heart. And I was beginning – just beginning – to learn about unconditional love. Learning to expect nothing. To put someone else's needs and difficulties before my own. The false dawn of four years earlier was now breaking.

Φ

But storm clouds were also gathering in the inner worlds and my unconscious mind saw them. In the second half of 1997 I dreamed of **my own death,** of **things 'being hidden'** and of **the loss of a key** (which was my personal symbol for Eve then). The I Ching described **a complete change ahead, a rivalry, a time of conflict and of 'modesty', meaning humility.** Unsurprisingly I became increasingly uneasy and knew there was going to be trouble...

You may think that I had already received considerable warnings – and indeed reassurances – of how this path would unfold, so perhaps I should have been more calm. But for one thing, many of the interpretations I have given could only have been made with hindsight and in several ways I was still an infant in this particular place of learning; I hadn't yet learned fully to trust the phenomenal accuracy of my guidance, or even to recognise clearly what *was* guidance. For another thing, when we are fully involved in actually living life we become caught up in all its events and feelings and thoughts so that it's extremely difficult to maintain any sort of 'detached overview'. Or maybe that's just me! In any case, it would certainly be a great problem over the next few years yet, my natural impatience and scepticism constantly doubting the teaching in the face of the sometimes horrible evidence of the real world. So in November 1997 I really messed up.

D   **24ᵗʰ November 1997: a short but immensely powerful dream. I saw clearly the numbers 200 and 1/6. Then I was with an A Level student named Tim Rivers outside the entrance of a sports centre I know well. I was going to go in here for a shower while my new, large house was being redecorated.**

Some of the symbolism here is archetypal: a river represents the rhythm of life, especially of the emotions, so it seems that my life was being cleansed (shower) and renewed (redecoration) perhaps at an 'advanced level' (large house). The numbers puzzled me for ages although I knew they represented time, as does 'Tim' of course; was I again looking forward to the year 2000 and the 'sixth' month as previous dreams had suggested? Spot on.

But events rapidly overtook these thoughts as just a few days later, in this very sports centre, I met an attractive young woman, Nell; and in my very unsettled state of mind – there had been further upsets with Eve recently – this was enough to provoke a split in our relationship. The reality of this was so dreadfully painful for us both, however, that we were back together within three weeks. How very forgiving she was. But the writing was now on the wall as I had let her down for the second time because of my impatience for security. A week later I dreamed of someone close to me being a murderer (was this in fact me?) and my New Year I Ching reading of 5ᵗʰ January 1998 described the year ahead as being one of **"Revolution"**.

Surely not by coincidence, I decided at about this time to learn Reiki healing. I have described how I was involved for a while with spiritual healing in my youth but life had taken other directions and I hadn't pursued it (partly because I was afraid of my own ego getting in the way). Now I really felt that I wanted to be involved in this area again. I thought, of course, that I would be doing it in order to help others; but as things turned out I was going to need it pretty soon just for myself! An odd dream at the end of December 1997 had referred to a healing course and suggested an unfamiliar name that I recognised a week or so later when I was looking for a teacher. So I completed Level One of the training in January then Level Two in April 1998 – this detail will prove very significant later.

On the anniversary of my first marriage, another dream pointed the way ahead.

D   27th **January 1998: After several frustrations at a restaurant, I left but had difficulty driving properly, and for a while was on the wrong side of the road. Then I got my seatbelt on, cleared my head and settled down, turning at a major junction onto a clear, open road. 'Oasis' were playing on the radio and I knew that something important was 'just 2 m ahead'.**

The restaurant scenes show that I am not receiving the nourishment I want. Setting out to find a different way, I make mistakes and have trouble settling down; but I can sense clarity, security and peace (an oasis), and better days ahead. '2 m' seemed to look forward two years to the millennium, or 2000 (again). Then the springtime of 1998, days after my Reiki training and three years after starting out on my new path, heralded in one night two of the most terrifying dreams I have ever had.

D   24th **April 1998: I was at my parents' old house looking out over the garden, although it seemed very much like my own garden. A large and aggressive poodle appeared on a rockery and chased my cat Angie away. I ran to the front of the house and later she returned, frightened but unhurt.**

Then I was driving into the grammar school I had attended as a boy. But somebody else was driving out fast and I had to reverse suddenly – my brakes didn't work properly and I knew I was in great danger. At length I went back into the school grounds and to my office. But everything had been moved around and I wasn't even sure it was the right place. Moreover, my bicycle, which I'd left locked up, had been vandalised, both wheels and the chain stolen.

I awoke with a heavy and sick feeling, knowing with total clarity that I was going to lose Eve (Angie represented her because I used to call her 'Angel'), my life hitting the rocks, suffering reverses and being rearranged, a 'cycle' ended. Perversely, we seemed to have been quite happy at this time and I, at least, was really beginning to feel a depth of spiritual love that I hadn't known before. But it all happened one week after the dream. She walked away. She had met someone else. I couldn't blame her.

Well, on one level this was one of those important but eventually broken love affairs, with all its pleasures and sorrows, which so many people experience. Even when they don't work out, we are enriched by them. And I think I always knew that this relationship, albeit that it lasted two and a half years, could not be long term in the real everyday world. We were very different personalities and I was often very unsettled by our circumstances – I had after all looked for alternatives and maybe it was I who unconsciously provoked the end.

But it was much, much more than that. In trying to find my 'new spiritual path', it was essential for me to learn a new way of relating to others and embrace a higher awareness of what love means. This meant literally abandoning my 'self', confronting my own needs and desires and learning to let go of them instead of believing *that someone else could satisfy them*. So I had to meet Eve, had to love her and had to lose her, if I was to grow. The devastation that I felt in 1998 was the inevitable breaking up and cleansing out of the old self. I would eventually emerge with a little more patience and a little more understanding of others' difficulties, not to mention a sound lesson about personal integrity.

But the real reason for telling this story is something quite different. In 1998 I was in quite a bad way for a while. Yet I survived and grew stronger. I can never know how much I owed at this time to the care and support of 'higher spiritual forces' (angels? guides?) but I was certainly aware of somehow being loved and protected. Reiki healing also helped to stabilise me; why had I suddenly decided to learn it just a few months before? Throughout these three years it is undeniable that I had been receiving a stream of 'guidance' (and I have only described a fraction of the experiences), despite my own doubts. It seemed that I was being warned of troubles, reassured of my safety, and even given details of how the path would unfold ahead of me.

Nigel Peace

Once we set out on such a journey, there are signposts to guide the way.

III. *Signposts*

So far most of my inner experiences had been in the form of dreams, perhaps because I was still finding my way relatively unconsciously. But from now on other signs and omens began to play a greater part as I became more aware of the meaningfulness of life's events and was more deliberate in my search for understanding. You might say "Well, if you look for signs of course you'll think you see them." The response to this, naturally, is: "You won't see anything if you don't look."

I do concede that one can be silly about this if one is not careful – not every observation is a sign and not every apparent sign is helpful. Perspective and context are everything. Above all, surely we must never abandon personal responsibility for our own progress; we must exercise our free will and wisdom as best we can and make our own decisions if any one step forward is to be a genuine human advance. (Sorry, angels.)

Having made these high-flown remarks, I admit that I did get quite silly about it all for a while. For the record, over the next four year period I noted over a thousand car registrations (an average of nearly five per week) and about two hundred and fifty other 'significant signs' (one per week); I read the I Ching on average every three weeks and recorded as important an average of one dream per week. To be fair, a large proportion of the signs and readings were in the first year after May 1998 when I was in emotional pieces and needed help – any help going. I was looking for divine guidance. I found it too. Many signs (often in clusters of four or five on a single day) did help me at least in the sense that I felt reassured that I hadn't lost my way and that ultimately 'all would be well'. Despite my sadness, I never lost my optimism – I was beginning to have faith in the purposefulness of life.

However, I also began to realise that many signs, readings and even dreams were simply reflecting back to me my own state of mind; in a literal sense, I was creating them. This is why I now know how important it is to share these phenomena with others who can offer another perspective and help keep a balance (though it may be rare to find such a sensitive, kind and perceptive friend who doesn't think you're barking mad). Sometimes, for example, an I Ching reading would make little sense or two readings might appear to contradict each other. Surely this was because my inner mind was confused or I had not prepared myself properly or was too impatient for a definite answer. But one has to be brutally honest with oneself to know this at the time! Nor do such unhelpful readings invalidate the I Ching, and the same goes for other mystical experiences.

This path is not easy to follow, yet that is all part of the wonder and beauty of being human. So it is all the more wonderful when sometimes the clouds break and a shaft of bright light reveals exactly where we are...

D   **10th June 1998: I arrived at school on a bicycle, on a Saturday. When I put the brakes on they stuck and I fell off, part of the handlebars also coming loose. But I wasn't hurt. I mended the bike quickly and rode on, everything fine now. Someone else was arriving just behind me, also on a bicycle. I felt happy and could hear beautiful music from inside the school where people were rehearsing for a concert.**

Clearly, at this point in my emotional 'cycle' there was a 'break', a loss of control and an upset. But the dream told me that basically I was fine; moreover, a new relationship ('someone following') was on the way in due course. Things were as they should be – it was all part of the learning ('rehearsing') experience. In fact, the previous night I had dreamed of being at school at four o'clock on a Friday – the end of the weekly cycle with a period of rest ahead – and the later dream seemed to be taking this a stage further.

S   **11th June 1998: The day after the dream, *and while thinking about it*, I saw the car registration LUC 363. In the Gospel of Luke, chapter 3 verse 6 reads "All mankind shall see God's deliverance..." I read this as a Bible reference because my son's name is Luke and his mother is French, so she would spell his name in the French way. Therefore this seemed to me to be equivalent to my earlier observations of LUK – E plates!**

At this time my Reiki teacher was being wonderfully supportive and indeed gave me much healing, which I could certainly feel within me even at a distance from her. She suggested that I now learn Level Three. This was much sooner than is normal – the traditional way is to allow a considerable period of adjustment or 'apprenticeship' between the levels. But she felt that I was ready and that I needed it, as it would open me up to more powerful healing energy.

S   29ᵗʰ June 1998: I had to travel over a hundred miles to see her, but immediately I set out I saw the car registration 698 DAN. I read this as the Book of Daniel, chapter 6 verse 9 and following verses. Here, Daniel is cast into the lion's den, a test of his faith, and the king said to him: "Thy God... will deliver thee." Then when I eventually arrived at my destination, outside my teacher's house was a car with registration A11 RYT!

Many would see such 'signs' as fatuous, a grasping at spiritual straws. But when they are seen in their context and in conjunction with the dreams, when they are given a position in the continuum of one's inner experience, and when *they are consistent with each other* as these were, they offer much stronger support than straws. I felt positively reassured that I was on track, doing the right things and would get through my present crisis safely. The Reiki training was indeed hugely helpful; I immediately felt a better balance of the turbulent energy within me. There were still some very bad days, but I recovered from them more quickly. I was getting stronger.

Nonetheless I still felt pretty detached from the real world, living inside my head, still emotionally fragile. This can be a dangerous state to be in. On the one hand, you may be actively riding the waves of the inner stream of consciousness – but what about your work and responsibilities back here on Earth? Yes, there were moments when I feared for my own sanity and seriously considered giving up on all this 'spiritual stuff'. At just such a moment, another experience shocked me to the core.

S   7th August 1998: I watched a 'Cadfael' television play in which trial by Bible was depicted. This was a method used by the medieval Church to learn the 'higher truth' in legal cases where the evidence was inconclusive; after prayerful preparation, a high churchman would open the Bible at random and take whatever text his fingers touched as the judgement. I immediately felt the powerful inner energy, concentrated in the solar plexus, which I have come to associate with spiritually significant moments (I have had these feelings all my life but they were becoming stronger now and especially after the Reiki training). So later that night I prepared my mind and performed a 'trial' of the question: "Am I on a proper spiritual path?" The text I touched was the Gospel of John, chapter 12 verse 37: "In spite of the many signs he had shown them, they still would not believe him."

Ouch! This felt like a direct reprimand to me for my doubts and lack of faith. It was as if my spiritual guides were saying "Look, young chap, we're working our socks off here to give you more guidance than anyone has a right to expect, and you're not even sure if you're on the right path?" There have since been many such moments when it seems very difficult to deny the presence of an intelligent, personal guiding force. (But I still try.)

Meanwhile my own mind continued to present me with a series of important dreams which helped me to remain calm and forward-looking. Two in particular seemed to go further and offer specific yet enigmatic clues.

D   24th August 1998: I was at a sports centre watching Eve do cleaning work. It was a quiet evening and I was waiting for something. I couldn't understand why there were two swimming pools side by side. A man in black was helping her for a while but then he left. At closing time she came towards me but then I saw another woman enter the building and begin, apparently, to check the notice boards. A group of people then started to gather in a nearby room for a meeting.

I had already recognised that this was a 'cleansing' period and that, in part, had been Eve's purpose in my life. But it was less than four months since our separation and perhaps I was still hoping for her return; the dream told me there had to be a 'closure'. (Incidentally, her relationship with 'the other man' later broke up – in the dream, she separated from 'the man in black'.) Now, if water represents emotion then a pool must be a relationship, and the fact that there were two here again suggested that someone new would come into my life (there would be a 'meeting'). Clearly, there were things here that I had to take 'notice' of! In fact, the meeting was two years away – and with a quite incredible link to this dream.

D   **27th August 1998: In a bar, I asked for whisky but the careless barman put water in it. I decided not to make a fuss but accept it. Then I was on a trip to visit George Bernard Shaw's house, exploring rooms which I hadn't seen before. There was a garden outside, but unkempt and needing a lot of work doing to it. I heard an alarm and managed to get out through a fire exit. Then I was returning home, hitch-hiking, when a bus stopped for me – it was going to Victoria, exactly where I wanted to go and just 200 yards from where I had started. Later, I found myself in a new car and driving through Edgware.**

So I realised that I was not going to receive what, at this time, I was still hoping for. I had to let go and look further ahead to new experiences (I had visited Shaw's house with Eve). There was more reconstruction yet to do! But I would 'escape' from this danger, receive help and achieve 'victory' (a great pun). The dream again suggested the year 2000. Just two years later, in August 2000, I would be driving through Edgware to visit Alice.

Φ

At this time, several other dreams kept repeating the symbol 'four' or sometimes 'four plus four', presumably a time period. I began to wonder if I was getting a sense of the overall length of my 'training course' (somehow seeing far into the future to a time of resolution and a more peaceful life?). For example:

D   **19th September 1998: I was a boy preparing for morning Assembly at school. I had four gold rings and dropped one of them but then retrieved it. People were laughing at me because I couldn't find a seat, but then the Headmaster spoke up for me, people applauded and I got to my seat after all.**

I awoke with a great sense of clarity from this. Again it pointed to a meeting (assembly) and my recovery from a position of weakness – although the 'four', if a time period, suggested the summer of 1999 rather than 2000. This confused me for quite a while.

However, the greatest effect of this particular dream was a real feeling of encouragement and almost congratulation (in contrast to the previous month's telling off) as if from a high spiritual source (a 'master'). This would happen again a handful of times later. I was beginning to distinguish between different 'levels' of guidance, as if I was accessing states of consciousness which are of different depth. It is difficult to explain how because it is so subjective, but sometimes there was a greater sense of 'contact', a deeper feeling of peace afterwards, a longer-lasting effect. There would be many moments when I unmistakably felt that *it was not my mind at all at work but that I was receiving something from outside myself.* This experience is humbling. Alternatively, the truth may be far more simple... Consider another example:

S   **My own pain during this year had made me much more sensitive to others and deeply aware of the pain that I had caused others in the past. I tried in my small way to make good by writing letters to certain people, expressing my sorrow and asking forgiveness, though I didn't receive any replies! So one night, very upset, I made a heartfelt prayer for forgiveness. The next morning as I left home I saw the car registration – 981 DAN which I read as the Book of Daniel, chapter 9 verse 8 and one more verse: "We... are covered in shame. We have** sinned… You forgive us…" This was a direct response to my prayer – how could I have created it myself?

Whatever the truth of this, as that year ended I felt much stronger due in no small way to a series of signs (mainly Bible references such as New Testament healings and miracles, or Job's deliverance in the Old Testament) and dreams telling me that things were 'about to happen'. Sometimes I was blessed with the long view.

D   **19th December 1998: I was driving a small bus up a long steep hill. At the top were two sharp turns, difficult to manoeuvre – but I managed it, felt good, and then drove right up to and inside a larger bus! Waiting there was a friend of mine named Claire. She had to leave soon but before she went I gave her some money that I'd changed for her; it was two thousand French francs.**

This was describing the struggle of my new way of life but promising eventual transformation to something better (a bigger bus!) and to 'clarity'. There would be more twists and turns yet, though – perhaps two changes of direction? (Yes, and one of them would have a French connection.) Again the year 2000 was explicitly indicated. But this seemed a long way off – after all, 1999 was only just dawning.

S   **As if in sympathy, my car odometer which had been stuck on zero for two months suddenly started working again of its own accord on the 1st of January!**

IC   **My I Ching reading for the year ahead saw "The Abysmal" leading to "Deliverance".**

The New Year heralded a flurry of psychic activity. In the first month there were nine memorable dreams, including one about **rehearsals being over and the school play about to start** (harking back to the dream of 10th June 1998). Signs also came thick and fast, twenty this month, ranging from Bible references such as **M 106 ARK ("prepare the way")** to … **JOY,** to **my car mirror being**

broken (which I took to suggest that I must not look back!). I was sure now that an important meeting was imminent – in fact there were two.

On the 10th of January I had dreamed of **being at a school art exhibition where I saw ten paintings**. Ten days later I was invited to an exhibition by the mother of one of my son's friends and herself a professional sculptress and artist; not only did we develop a good friendship, from this point I found myself drawn more and more into the world of art and of alternative perspectives on reality. This would be very rewarding, not least in beginning to appreciate things for what they were and becoming less judgemental!

Then there was a small collection of very strange signs:

S   **1st February 1999:**

(1) There was a short, and very rare, power failure at home which reset all my clocks to zero. It reminded me of a dream on 15th August 1998 in which I had met a sculptress and then seen a clock being reset to zero.

(2) I received some unsolicited 'psychic' junk mail which promised me "a new future" due to start on 13th March and a period of special good fortune "lasting 88 days" (provided that I sent some money…!) This in turn seemed linked to a dream on the 19th August 1998 in which I'd watched my old school being reconstructed (i.e. 'new relationship') and later seen someone wearing a sports shirt with the number 88 on it. Yes, such mail is generally rubbish, but read on…

(3) Almost the first car seen that day had the number M 292 ARK which reads as "…take up your bed and walk…" This describes a healing and represents new movement.

A few days later I met Dawn (with a French Caribbean background) and we were definitely attracted to each other, although our first real 'date' together wasn't until… er, the 13th of March! (It would be the middle of summer before the '88' made sense.) It was a pretty stormy relationship; we were both strong personalities and both emerging from emotional crises. But there were also wonderful times and *I began to feel really alive again*, my self-confidence restored and the ties to the past loosened. I believe that just by coming together we did much to heal each other's pain, and if this was the 'purpose' of our meeting then we can be grateful.

D   But almost as soon as my dreams had finished predicting her arrival, they began to warn me of conflict ahead and against believing that this relationship had greater significance than it actually did. Already in February I dreamed of things being turned upside down, of missing the right turning in my car, of being on a hill in a war zone. In March I missed a train, and in April my car crashed again on the A41; I also discovered a bomb in a hotel!

IC   Also in early April, an I Ching reading for our new relationship promised "Obstruction" leading to the need to "Work on What Has Been Spoiled".

S   Then on the 15th of May my car's odometer stuck on zero again!

This really wasn't what I wanted to be hearing. Yes, there were a handful of painful scenes with Dawn, but on balance I was feeling so much more, well, balanced. It's hard to accept that some encounters may have a very specific purpose but then must be left behind. However, my guidance was absolutely unequivocal.

D   20th May 1999: I was on a ship about to leave port and in a queue to get my ticket processed. I was jostled and lost a bag. Then I saw Dawn sitting nearby. I went through the ticket control but a friend said this was the wrong way and I should go back. I found myself out on deck where a steward dressed all in white gave me a white satin rope and urged me towards the stern by pulling on the other end of the rope. The ship was now on the point of leaving and the steward was insistent that I should get off; he kept encouraging me to jump and even got into the water himself to show me that it wasn't too deep...

The warning could not have been more clear: I had to change direction before I got 'in too deep' – it even seemed (the steward being all in white) as though I was being offered angelic help!

D   Five days later another dream promised a 'transformation' ahead and again featured the number four, and three days after this I dreamed of being 'half-way through an eight-ball over' in a cricket match.

This seemed to link with the earlier dream about the number '88' (the eight being repeated as if for emphasis). For the first time I now felt the very clear intuition that learning 'the new way' was to be an eight-year path, which I was now half way through – it was just four years since the decision to end my marriage.

IC   An I Ching reading in early June declared that this was "the moment to turn back" and to "bite through" (take decisive action). A further birthday reading a week later yielded Hexagram 36: "Darkening of the Light".

S   Later the same day, on a picnic, I got a splinter in one eye and needed hospital treatment!

Obviously, I wasn't seeing things clearly… Or rather, I saw but did not respond, despite the psychic evidence being absolutely overwhelming. In the next couple of weeks a further **I Ching reading yielded the self-explanatory Hexagram 39: "Obstruction", I dreamed of driving the wrong way down the A41 with Dawn, and almost everywhere I looked I seemed to see the car registration H – ELL!** The trouble is, I actually *was* becoming more loving so I was more prepared than in the past to 'let things go', to be accepting of difficulties, to be understanding. Perhaps I thought I could change everything. I couldn't. It all ended very badly within a month and yet again I felt very hurt – this really was a very unhealthy pattern!

On the other hand, as if my inner consciousness (or the spirit world?) were breathing a great sigh of relief, there were strong and immediate reassurances for me.

D   20th July 1999: a grand and formal event was about to start at school in the Great Hall and there were many well-dressed influential people there. I was on the balcony, feeling rather lonely and unsure of myself, not knowing where to stand, so I took up a modest position in a back corner. There was a ceremonial entrance by many dignitaries led by a high churchman, a 'holy man'. They came in at the far end, walked past almost the whole crowd and stopped in front of me; the churchman blessed me by baptising my forehead with holy water. It was a truly wonderful feeling and I fell to my knees in joy and humility.

The extraordinary feeling persisted when I woke up as if I was living in a lighter, clearer world – it was a very *real* experience. But where had it come from and why? For several days in my everyday life I had been in emotional pain not to mention mental confusion (thinking that "I'd got it all wrong again"). Set as it was in school, I knew the dream concerned my loving relationships but this was *far* more than a self-therapeutic "Ah well, never mind, things will get better eventually…". This felt like a direct spiritual message, from beyond my own mind, that despite messing up I was on the right path and learning what I had to learn. And there was even more:

S   20th July 1999: When I came downstairs the morning after this dream I found my front door open (I have no idea how, it had never happened before and hasn't ever since). On the mat was some junk mail offering me "The secrets of spiritual power". As it was a lovely day I went straight out into the garden, where a butterfly came to rest on a bush inches from my face – it was a Ringlet, with just four rings on its wings.

In themselves, these events may seem insignificant but their synchronicity with the dream is amazing. The mail echoed the dream's feeling of spiritual blessing while an open door represents opportunity and progress. The butterfly was pretty rare for my area; a ring naturally suggests emotional security, but moreover here there were four – exactly as I had dreamed the previous September when a boy in the same assembly hall at school was trying to find his place. Then to top it all, I realised that today was my parents' wedding anniversary.

Φ

Looking back over so many strange experiences, I have often thought that either I am completely mad or I am one of the most fortunate men alive, given the extraordinary degree of 'guidance' I receive. I'm fairly sure that it's not the former, because so many signs, dreams and readings have proved phenomenally consistent and accurate. But the question has then to be asked whether I am also one of the most stupid men alive, since I have so often ignored or failed to understand the 'advice'. Supposing for a moment that we are in fact cared for and supported by loving spirit beings – mine must be the most frustrated in all Heaven.

My only defence is that I'm human. Surely I can't be expected to understand all these things or have a calm, clear overview of life's course while I'm actually embroiled in it. I never had an angel stand right in front of me, wings rippling, beatific light shining from his eyes, telling me to my face How Things Are. One has to work things out for oneself. (Incidentally, I have often wondered whether all those Biblical accounts of angelic messages were in fact experiences much like mine – perhaps dreams - but couched in the religious language of the time.) Then even when I do understand the signposts, I sometimes persist in making wrong turnings because of my weakness or wilfulness or perhaps emotional neediness. I behave like a small child in this great school of ours, extremely curious yet often defying my excellent teachers, falling over and grazing my knees...

The important thing, however, is to pick yourself up and try again. And if indeed I was four years into an eight-year cycle, my half-term report couldn't have been *all* bad. The reliability of so many of these marvellous experiences encouraged my awareness and sense of purpose, my belief in the spiritual path I had embarked upon.

The existence of meaningful signposts means that one is on the right road!

And the small child gradually does start to grow up. Every day I was trying a little more deliberately to be more understanding and loving towards others, and the awareness of my own mistakes taught me to respond more kindly to others'. As the journey unfolded I was becoming more conscious of it as a coherent whole and recognising that it was leading to some real resolution. My dreams in particular were becoming more integrated and I was recognising cross-references between them as if I was doing a fiendishly difficult jigsaw puzzle: hesitantly at first with several errors, but then as the picture begins to emerge the pieces fall into place more easily.

I was also learning fast to trust my intuition and my feelings, to appreciate and express the non-rational, beginning to 'know things', to sense the 'energies' around people or situations, to feel the 'quality' of an event. Perhaps because of this, I was now beginning to have more experiences that seemed related to 'angels' or 'spirits'. I had rejected Spiritualism twenty-five years before, but for all my scepticism I couldn't help the powerful feeling that a loving and intelligent presence was often with me. In particular, the night before the solar eclipse in 1999 I am convinced that I met with a particular, individual spirit.

D   **11ᵗʰ August 1999: This took the form of a dream but its immediacy, vibrancy and depth gave it a different quality to any I had had before. A man appeared and clearly identified himself, using symbolism, as Eve's father. (He had died before I met her.) He showed me that my relationship with her was indeed over (I had been thinking about her a lot since the separation from Dawn) but that she had been 'the key' to my**

new way of living. Another beautiful relationship lay ahead, and again the number four was stressed.

I awoke stunned, clearly understanding the message given, and the 'presence' stayed with me throughout the rest of the night. All the same, I was still feeling emotionally raw and at such times it is difficult to hear that 'happiness' may be another four years away! Further dreams and signs kept coming of course but they were not very specific, offering general encouragement that I was going in the right direction, warning me against being impatient, insisting that I let go of the past, that I needed to let my wounds heal… This was probably very sensible, but I have always been impatient and found it extremely difficult to accept such lulls in life, times of consolidation.

Still, I kept myself busy and finally managed to complete the internal redecoration of my new home. The new look had beautiful colour and much more light than before. I also began a general clearout, which left a lot of space in cupboards and on shelves. As the end of the year approached, I realised that all this activity in the everyday world represented two important things about my inner world: firstly, there was a recognition of how far I had come and how much had been achieved; secondly, I was making space and giving up control so that my life could be more fully shared with another. Where was this leading? My mind demanded facts and eventually got them.

D   **28th November 1999: I climbed very fast the 52 steps of a circular stone tower, like in a castle. Then on 30th November I dreamed of repeatedly hearing "six"; thinking this meant years, I tried to calculate the number of days and kept getting "two thousand". I awoke hearing in my head the Strangelove song "I Will Burn".**

The first dream seemed to promise improvement for me, perhaps in one year's time (52 weeks)? Clearly, my unconscious mind kept working on the problem and came up with the year 2000, as had been suggested several times before; in the event, I met Alice in the sixth month of that year. What was more extraordinary however, although I couldn't possibly recognise it then (and just as well), was that my mind was already looking *beyond* that relationship – it would end, and I would get 'burned', just before my fifty-second birthday!

Then, on the day that I finished the work in my house, I got the full picture.

D **24ᵗʰ December 1999: I was getting changed in a school building, preparing for my second football match. Outside, there was a pitch marked on the playground with towers at each corner; a second pitch with similar towers was being prepared next to it. The other players were on a raised platform at one end so I went over, climbed the steps, and heard our coach giving an inspiring team talk. He pointed out the time to me – 2000 hours.**

So there was going to be 'change' and a second important relationship, presumably in the year 2000 (I think I really had got this message by now). It would be an improvement (up the steps) and inspirational. But I should see it within the overall pattern: a four-year cycle had been completed, another was under way.

As the new millennium dawned, a succession of spiritual events tumbling over each other in a ten-day period filled me with optimism. Dreams described me **'finding the solution to a difficult problem'**, having **'proof in 2000'** and the answer being related to **'art'**, having a **'second chance'** and moving to **'a new land at junction eight'**, listening to **'The Ring Cycle'** and again finding **'eight as two fours'** important. In the daytime, car registrations all referred to **healings or miracles or preparation**. The very first car I saw on the 1ˢᵗ of January had the number **P33ACE**! Then some junk mail informed me that it was **"Time to change your life"**. What I didn't understand, however, was that amidst all this there were also dreams about **'disruption'** or **'reversal'** to be dealt with. My New Year reading was just as enigmatic.

IC **8ᵗʰ January 2000: "How will this year develop for me?" yielded Hexagram 19, "Approach". This is generally one of the**

most fortunate hexagrams in the book, the judgement describing a time when many things have happened and been remedied, thus a time of greatness can approach. But the moving lines of this reading spoke of 'people being obstructive' and of one's place being 'inappropriate'. Great restraint, integrity and inner belief were going to be demanded of me. Given this, the result was Hexagram 11: "Advance", a time of peace and progress.

Putting this all together, I reasoned that a period of happiness in my emotional and spiritual life was about to dawn this year – probably a meeting with someone special – but that things would not go particularly smoothly. Then, when did they ever? One does not learn without challenges. I was going to have to be strong and patient for a while yet.

I prayed for 'angelic guidance' about this.

D   21st January 2000: This was another dream, like that in August, of a different quality. I was visited by a man who simply told me that his name was Jamie and then said: "Praise be the Lord. We're nearly there." I also saw an image of three people standing as if in a triangle.

About thirty years earlier I had visited a psychic artist who told me that I had a spirit guide who had been a Presbyterian minister named Jamie McIntyre (he drew a sketch of him for me). But I hadn't thought much about this since then, nor had there apparently been any other 'contact' with him. Was he now reappearing in my life to reassure me?

And was he warning me about a love triangle?

IV. *Grand Alignment*

I couldn't say that I was happy at this time. When you decide to live with an open heart, you're going to get hurt. Well, any sort of real learning can be painful because it involves real change, and there had been plenty of that in the last few years. Moreover, this sort of path can be lonely. You may reasonably be thinking that with all the clues and reassurances I had been receiving, surely by now I should have been able to live with some equanimity. It's a fair point! But in the everyday world with all its chores and challenges, responsibilities and stress, it's difficult to live with that heightened consciousness. It's like when you have a really heavy cold: your head throbs, your limbs ache, your throat's on fire and your eyes are streaming; and even though you *know* that "it's just a cold and I'll be better next week", that doesn't stop you feeling awful!

On the other hand, I had at least by now absorbed the I Ching's philosophy that 'life is change'. Nothing remains the same for there are cycles of increase and decrease, and we know them better the more mindful we are of our lives. So, yes, I knew there would be turning points ahead (and how); but the hardest lesson for me, one who is naturally impatient and used to making things happen, is that sometimes there is nothing to be done but (in the book's words) retreat, maintain one's inner belief, and wait for the right time… And as if I'd received all the guidance I needed, my inner world went very quiet for several months. It's not that I didn't dream or see signs, but they were fewer and usually related to more prosaic matters such as my career.

There was the odd reference again to 'change', 'a period of four', 'solving a puzzle' and to 'art'. And then Jamie returned.

D   **9th March 2000: I am a young man, not feeling very confident, but pleased to be setting out from home in my own car. Later, I park the car at the junction with Turner Road, outside number 52, and wonder what's going to happen next. My mobile 'phone rings in my pocket – it's a Scottish man I met recently, a therapist, who is checking to see that I'm all right.**

The dream described me well, a young student of the spiritual way gradually finding my feet. Both 'junction' and 'Turner' suggested change approaching, and the number 52 harked back to the important dream of the previous November. (It's also worth mentioning that in this dream, as in very many others, I was aware of 'someone' being with me all the time although I couldn't tell who it was – there would be a spectacular explanation of this four months later.) I sort of associated the 'therapist' with the Scottish church minister, Jamie, supposedly one of my 'spirit guides' who has been mentioned earlier. But I didn't take this thought seriously – until December 2003.

Pretty soon, things really began to hot up.

S . **2nd May 2000: I saw the unusual car registration 1.1GHT. Later I listened to a moving radio play about Barnes Wallis wooing Mollie Bloxham; it struck me as peculiar because my mother's name is Mollie, she lived in a village called Bloxham, whereas Wallis' fiancée lived in Hampstead extremely close to where I was then driving! This couple's relationship was very difficult for two and a half years, but then they were married for fifty-four years; again it would turn out that I was picking up 'clues' about my own future life.**

S **3rd May: another unusual personalised number V11RTU followed by … EVE, … TAO, a different … EVE again and then … 579 DAN which refers to "the writing on the wall". ('Tao' means the path.)**

S **4th May: for some reason I didn't understand, the car M 106 ARK sounded its horn at me. The reference is to Christ's baptism. I then listened to another radio play which featured a baptism. Later this night there would be an extremely rare Grand Planetary Alignment in which six planets of our solar system plus our moon and the Sun formed up (the next similar alignment would be, significantly, in April 2002). The same evening I went to an art exhibition entitled (coincidentally, as it happens) Planet Dance by the artist Molly Ackerman where I** saw a very special abstract painting, which would become important to me and to my new relationship.

All of this gave me the very distinct feeling that a new beginning was just ahead with things 'falling into place'. Not only had I come to recognise such a cluster of small synchronicities as a definite signpost of being on the right track, there had been a whole series of experiences in recent years apparently pointing towards the summer of 2000. Now I really began to believe them.

D   **5th June 2000: This started as a normal dream, with me in a school which was being rebuilt. (You will recognise this symbolism now.) I received a message... Then Eve's father identified himself to me again and took me on a long journey to show me a place of almost unimaginable beauty where magnificent massive white buildings rose out of a calm mist. The roof of the building seemed to be in a Spanish style. As we climbed some steps I saw a portrait and an inscription on a nearby wall (but, infuriatingly, couldn't read it!). The 'dream' was very long and detailed; I was being given to understand that I should be prepared for a wonderful new start (at the end of August, I think). The 'key' I had lost would be rediscovered and a new cycle would begin. But I would have to resist 'threats' and be very loving.**

This was a very deep and 'far away' experience. For hours after waking I could still sense a presence with me and there was the very real feeling of a hand holding mine. This spirit had visited me the previous August, had referred then to a key and to a new relationship. As if to follow this up with more detail, there was another dream two nights later.

D   **7th June 2000: I was at a church I knew in my childhood, then with a woman and her husband Charles, setting out on a journey north. We should arrive by eight o'clock.**

This was more confirmation of going in the right direction (north) and of the overall pattern of eight years on my particular spiritual path (the church). I couldn't, of course, know then that Alice's husband's name was Charles…And if that's strange enough, you just won't believe this next bit.

S   **15th June 2000: As I went to sleep on the night before my birthday, I heard a sudden loud noise from my study. I discovered that the notice board on the wall, which had been stuck there for nearly five years, had fallen off for no apparent reason.**

I immediately remembered the dream of August 1998 about two pools, Eve and another woman checking notice boards, and a meeting… The very next evening I found that my son and my sculptress friend had arranged a surprise birthday party for me, the house decorated and wonderful food prepared. The centrepiece was **a fantastic homemade cake, which my friend had decorated with an I Ching Hexagram (though she had no idea what it meant) - it was 24: "Return".** Eve herself had been invited but didn't stay long, and there was just one guest whom I didn't know; this was Alice, an artist and the girlfriend of one of my friends. And this was exactly five years after that definitive dream at the point of ending my marriage.

This emotional and momentous evening had been foretold in so many ways, yet I still didn't quite realise what it meant! Later on I did get to talk with Alice and it was evident that we were attracted and had much in common; there was again that sense that we had somehow known each other a long time. But she was after all with someone else and although I knew the relationship was shaky I couldn't act improperly. In the next few weeks I found myself bombarded with car registrations referring to **miracles, dream interpretation (Daniel) and the parable of the sower ("some fell on good soil")**, and another of those junk mail envelopes proclaiming **"Look! I am making all things new."** I felt more confused than usual. There was undeniably a tide of Fate building up and my mind buzzed with psychic energy but didn't have a clue what to do with it. An I Ching reading didn't clarify things.

IC   7th July 2000: A question about the year ahead for me yielded Hexagram 6: "Conflict", which described a situation that one cannot win so one has to retreat. The outcome was Hexagram 12: "Hindrance".

Now as it happens this would be pretty accurate if one looked several months ahead, but it was neither helpful nor auspicious at the time. This is either an example of why one should not use the I Ching when one is feeling confused, or it was a lesson to me that I should accept what I had already been told (which, let's face it, was considerable) and not expect any more guidance about present events. It soon became obvious to both Alice and me, in telephone conversations, that we *were* indeed starting a relationship, that the energy between us was just too strong despite us both having reservations. When we eventually met again, we argued violently and then fell into each other's arms.

All the same, my mind was warning me of something.

S   13th July 2000: I sat in my garden reading a letter from Alice inviting me to dinner. As I did so, a large white spider appeared on the ivy near my head and began spinning a web.

D   14th July 2000: I had a long and cathartic nightmare in which I searched over and over again for food but every time was denied and dismissed by my mother.

It seems that I sensed some kind of emotional trap – the spider would become an important symbol of this relationship – and this encounter had awakened in me deeply-felt pain to do with the lack of 'nourishment' I had felt from several important women in my life. There had been a pattern of withdrawing love and of betrayal. Was I 'being warned' against this new relationship? But surely not, for this meeting had been predicted for five years and the signs had invariably been happy ones. Only in retrospect have I fully understood that it was the very depth of the encounter already that was making me aware of the precise emotional and spiritual issues that I had to learn to deal with on this path. *This was what needed to be healed.* I had to learn to trust, to forgive, and to love without condition. This relationship was going to offer me another opportunity. At the time, however, I just felt wretchedly confused and was beating myself up over my failure to understand! Then a remarkable thing happened.

S   **16ᵗʰ July 2000: Two young Mormons came to the door inviting me to discuss 'the family'. I normally have little time for their particular dogmas but something about them, or my state of mind, made me invite them in and we had a long and valuable talk about spiritual matters. At no time did they try to press their beliefs on me. We even discussed 'spirit encounters' and they felt that mine were genuine.**

When they left I felt calm and blessed, as if they had indeed been 'sent' to reassure me that what I was trying to do with my life was truly worthwhile. It was a reminder, too, that my complicated mind can all too easily lead me into error; I must not lose sight of my purpose or inner beliefs. Within days this new relative clarity was rewarded with three powerful dreams. Two made specific predictions, but the first described my entire journey and where it was leading.

This is probably my favourite of all the dreams I have ever had.

D   **25ᵗʰ July 2000: I find myself on a long journey, at first on a motorbike and then driving a coach, on uneven roads with difficult turns. I'm aware that there's someone beside me, navigating and encouraging me, and I seem to be doing quite well. The vehicle becomes a train running on tracks but the journey is taking a long time. Then I'm at the wheel of a large bus driving along narrow country roads in the dark; I've never been here before yet I seem to recognise the area from my dreams!**

There's definitely someone guiding me now, I can hear their voice. One of the mirrors gets broken and people in white overalls come on board to mend it; they're cheerful and friendly but I complain to them that I can't be expected to understand the difficult language they use – I have to concentrate on driving. We enter a village and I make a

mistake, veering off the road to follow a van which turned without signalling; I realise the problem quickly and turn back onto our road, apologising to my guide who says it's fine, not to worry.

But then there's a sharp right turn up a very steep hill with another left turn at the top – and I know that this heavy vehicle won't make it. I ask my guide's advice and he says: "You just have to do what you've done before." So I get out and climb the hill with a rope, pulling the vehicle up by sheer effort. At the top of the hill there are some people who briefly greet me before moving on; one of them is my father and I also notice an attractive young woman. I know there's not too far to go now and I'm about to meet my lover just up ahead. But first I go back to help a woman I know who has had a fall and been hurt.

Phew! The whole picture. I'm sure the meaning of the mostly archetypal symbols here is pretty obvious: life as a tricky journey of challenge, progress, mindfulness and sometimes mistakes. I was being told that with Alice I would have to draw on what I had learned before, would require the same determination and forbearance that I had needed before (with Eve). But there would be happiness and achievement. I was on 'the right track' and would reach 'the top of the hill'.

But the most wonderful aspect of the dream for me was the clearest indication yet that there are loving guides beside me all the way.

They even had a joke at my expense, coming on board to mend the broken mirror (one of my 'signs') and suggesting that I'd misunderstood what it meant. Well, I'm only human aren't I, and this spirit communication business *is* difficult. I was glad to 'meet' my father though we didn't make proper contact for another two years, and I didn't understand about the attractive young woman – until I met her a year later... The rest would also have to wait. There was life to be lived *now* and we cannot know our future, can we, when it depends upon how we live our present.

D   27th July 2000: I am taking a group of young people
including my son to a leisure centre, travelling in two coaches.
We have to go up a steep driveway with a difficult turn. The
woman driving one of the coaches is doing well but then, as
I'm outside guiding her, she suddenly feels unsure and
accelerates – the coach becomes an airplane, takes off, flies
vertically and is lost from sight. I have to supervise the other
children but am stricken with grief. Just as we're about to leave
the centre later, the other coach suddenly reappears safely. I
feel tremendous joy and relief.

This dream predicted that once again I might lose what is
most dear to me and be 'abandoned' again. But it was also a
powerful reminder that I must never lose my belief: **situations can
change suddenly and miraculously.**

D   29th July 2000: I was camping in my garden, listening to
the news. Someone said that everyone should go outside and
see the historic events. The sky was lit up by the fire of nine
missiles. It's as if a world war has broken out although I know
that we'll be safe because we have strong allies. One of my toes
is slightly hurt by shrapnel as I shelter by a fir tree, but in the
end there is little damage. Hearing a noise at my back gate, I
look over to see my cat Angie trying to climb back in.

The dream predicted both global and personal events of the
ninth month in the next year, and also echoed my dream of April
1998 in which my cat had been lost but then returned. In fact, days
after the terrorist attacks on America, Eve did indeed get back in
touch with me, having broken up with the lover who had replaced
me. It would be a challenge to my personal progress – but only a
hurt toe! For now I was feeling much more certain of my 'destiny'
with Alice, and before the relationship had even started properly I
seemed to know how it would unfold with difficulties, heartache,
loss and recovery. You might think that this should have put me off!
But this awareness simply helped me to recognise that we were
sharing a genuinely spiritual and purposeful path. Knowing this

helps one to keep a perspective beyond the transitory difficulties of this world. Then August brought a series of weird events, which convinced me that we were being encouraged and helped.

S   14th August 2000: I was driving one of Luke's friends home and as we set out I saw the car registration E 898 LUC – here, the parable of the sower is explained and it is said that "what is hidden will become known". Then the friend realised he'd left his 'phone behind and we had to go back; I couldn't help thinking to myself "This is deliberate, there's going to be another sign now." Sure enough, as we left home again the car L 421 UCE flashed its lights at me. The reference is "God has sent me to announce good news."

IC   19th August 2000: Feeling that I was now on the very brink of something huge, I asked the question "How will my life develop in the next few days?" Hexagram 64 is "Not Yet Fulfilled (or, Before Completion)" and the last hexagram in the book, representing the approach of an entirely new cycle, a transition from disorder to order. The moving lines urged me to remain steadfast and upright while enjoying life, for my goal would be fulfilled "in three years". "Rewards come from a great kingdom." The result is Hexagram 7: "Multitude" in which personal strength brings peace and good fortune. Time periods mentioned in the I Ching are not necessarily to be read literally – but this one was, for three years time would be eight years after 'setting out'…

S   26th August 2000: My new cooker was delivered – symbolically, the heart of the home's energy. Simultaneously I began to feel a huge rush of psychic energy pouring through me almost painfully (and it continued for five days). Later that afternoon I was pondering the problem of how to dispose of the old cooker when I heard a bell ringing outside; unbelievably, it was an old-fashioned 'rag and bone man' or scrap dealer – I hadn't seen one for many years. Problem solved instantly! A flurry of car registrations this week then referred to "transfiguration", "the glory of God" and "how great are God's signs".

Meanwhile, Alice and I had not seen each other for six weeks due to family holidays but then on the 1st of September we met again for dinner and became lovers. Her previous relationship was by now over and we felt free and happy. It was exactly as had been predicted by Eve's father.

Naturally, I then did an I Ching reading for the future of our new relationship.

IC   19th September 2000: Hexagram 64 is "Before Completion", exactly the same response I had received a month earlier. There was just one moving line, the sixth and the very last one in the book. A 'great task' is being undertaken and 'one approaches fulfilment'. While enjoying life there is still 'a need for steadfastness'. This time the outcome, while in harmony with the earlier one, was even more beautiful – Hexagram 40 is "Deliverance", the movement beyond danger when difficulties are resolved and the past forgiven.

Φ

All the signs and dreams and readings now seemed to have fallen into place. It was all coherent. I knew that I was where I should be and that the path was unfolding as it should. The rest of this year was happy – we spent a lot of time together, including a trip abroad to buy the painting that had so impressed me in May. We made new friends and explored art galleries, and quickly seemed to know each other very well, comfortable and at peace.

But it wasn't long before the underlying challenges began to surface in the real world. Most of them concerned Alice's family. She was separated from her husband, living independently and their children were quite grown up, but there were still close ties in the family and she came under pressure, sometimes quite overtly from these others, to give me up. At the same time, she herself felt uncomfortable about the changes in all these relationships now that we were becoming 'serious'. This became the most important and abiding difficulty for us, and we both had much to learn from the situation. It was at least clear to me that this was just what had been predicted by "not quite genuine" (November 1995), "obstructive people" and "inappropriate place" (January 2000), "resisting threats" (June 2000), "negative forces" (July 2000) – all readings made before our relationship had even started. It explained the "hill to be climbed" (July 2000) and the need for "restraint" (September 2000) on my part.

Alice needed me to be understanding, undemanding and simply loving, to draw upon all that I had been trying to learn these last five years or so. Sometimes I failed because I felt sidelined, like so often before, but because she was so very caring, her very awareness of my pain only made her more unsure. I had to try harder!

S   Car registrations at this time often seemed to refer to 'faith' (for example: ...797 LUC), to 'forgiveness' (...869 JON) and 'integrity' (...292 JOB).

D   I dreamed of things being stolen from my car (10th October), of a boy arriving at his new school but having to wait until Period 4 after a Break (8th November), of trees being cut down in my garden (2nd December) and of my garden path being broken up and the lawn ruined by a group of disruptive boys (21st December). The clincher was my car going backwards out of control while a friend drove off in another direction (12th January 2001).

IC   A New Year reading described "joyfully linked spirits" being confronted by "an adversary", a "turning away" and the "need for sincerity". The result was "Revolution".

The pressure was just too great, despite our love for each other. Alice felt torn apart by divided loyalties (one of her children simply said "It's him or me") and of course I felt rejected. We split up on the 15th of January and I spent most of the next week crying and in actual physical pain. Just what did God want of me? Hadn't I been through enough, tried hard enough, learned enough, only to lose already what had started to become perhaps the deepest relationship of my life? So what if the dreams and the signs and the readings had foretold this? Perhaps the achievement they also foretold was just wishful thinking…

Ah, but hang on, I managed to tell myself eventually – you can't take one without the other, accept the truth of the negative stuff but not of the positive. And you can't give up just because it's tough going. *It is the very nature of the spiritual path that our faith is constantly challenged. Our inner belief must be unswerving. Our love of truth must be absolute.* At this very low point, my unconscious again stepped in to assure me that despite all the difficulties there would be a happy outcome.

D   **21ˢᵗ January 2001: I was with others in a large, unfamiliar railway station, going somewhere important. I got separated from the others and felt anxious, then went down two floors in a lift. But then I found 'the right place' and met characters from the TV programme 'The Good Life'; it was about 4:15 pm.**

IC   **21ˢᵗ January 2001: The response for "Our future?" was Hexagram 35, "Progress".**

D   **23ʳᵈ January 2001: I was embarking on a large and beautiful ship for an ocean voyage, and there was going to be a reunion with my friend Alan. I was part of a big family group but we became separated. The men's cabins were along narrow confusing corridors and were uncomfortable. But then while having dinner later, a very senior officer dressed all in white came to say that our accommodation had been "upgraded to number eight", which was a very high standard.**

Both dreams described my sense of loss and the difficulties still to be faced (separation, confusing paths and uncomfortable places). But this was a great journey that would lead, after a period of eight, to achievement and happiness – a good life! Incredibly, it would be almost precisely April 15ᵗʰ (4:15) in two years time that I would know the reality of this. Meanwhile, I would be reunited with

Alice, who has the same initials as my friend Alan. The relationship obviously wasn't over if it was to 'progress'. It is interesting to note the contrast between the adventure of this voyage and the warning of the voyage in May 1999 – *and just who are these people in white?*

S   **25th January 2001: I lost a contact lens but after a long search found it again. Later that day Alice telephoned and we agreed to meet in two days time.**

S   **27th January: In driving about fifty miles across London today I only saw one significant number plate and that was when I was temporarily lost: ...19 JON. (Jonathan is my son's middle name.) This reads "The light shines on in the dark and the darkness never extinguishes it." When I met Alice for dinner later, one of the things we talked about was Luca Pacioli, a fifteenth century monk who interests me. Leaving the restaurant I saw L 287 UCA: "The angel of the Lord came upon them... tidings of great joy."**

We got back together that night and I was at peace again, in the right place. It wasn't over yet. The next three months were again happy. I recognised in Alice a beautiful soul, perhaps struggling to express herself fully, and I grew a little more gentle, a little less self-interested. Our relationship was very close and our lives full of good energy – she started a wonderful new job and I was rebuilding the paths in my garden! So I was inclined to shrug off renewed warnings.

D   **27th February 2001: I had organised a Careers event at school. It went well although afterwards there was something of a disturbance caused by a woman; she fell and I helped her up. My mother was waiting to take me home in a car but I said I had a responsibility to stay longer and would be home "in one hour". I then saw that almost the whole site was being demolished and reconstructed. This made me very anxious but I was aware of people with me, protecting me and assuring me that the new building would be much better. Three young people became aggressive towards me, then another younger** person too, but I made them back off and they disappeared. I went inside to a café where people were friendly towards me; a seat was given up for me because someone was coming soon who wanted to meet me. A woman was telling the others that a man had abused her but that I had dealt with him. At the end of the event I heard happy music being played; a woman sat at the control deck and nearby was her son, reading a History book.

IC   6ᵗʰ April 2001: "What is the future for this relationship?" Hexagram 43 is "Breakthrough" but, for the first time in my experience, five of the six lines were moving. It read like a complete account of the relationship from the 'difficulty at the beginning' to the 'negative influences' and 'obstructions', ending with 'the struggle is not hopeless, do not be deflected'.

S   The next day I heard a radio play in which a character consulted the I Ching (the only time I've ever heard this in a drama) and obtained exactly the same Hexagram!

At the time of this dream I was in fact organising just such an event at school for a few days later, but nothing untoward happened; it would be the day of a similar event *one year later* that the real demolition began. Helping a woman who had fallen echoed the similar event near the end of the important dream in July 2000. I took the confrontational young people to be Alice's family (who would in fact eventually change their attitude). I also realised that 'home in one hour' probably meant some resolution in a year's time, but I couldn't have known that in fact it referred to exactly one year after the decisive Careers event, when indeed there would be an important meeting with a woman who had suffered abuse and when another young person would confront me. But at the end of the day, things would be 'under control'...?

Again, I was seeing *two years ahead* to the end of the eight-year cycle, when I would be 'coming home'. Similarly, the I Ching was describing the 'responsibilities' of my path with Alice in the meantime. Its outcome was Hexagram Four.

Two weeks later, Alice's family again put pressure on her and she just couldn't cope with the division of loyalty (despite a graphic dream of her own the night before, clearly warning her that she was being denied her own life). A mother will – and surely should – always choose her children, right or wrong. So for now and for many months afterwards our emotional life was very turbulent. The love that we felt for each other would pull us back together and for a while we'd be happy and close; then within weeks she would begin to feel that the risk was too great and would withdraw. She wasn't only protecting herself; she knew that I was not receiving the nourishment I needed and wanted me to be 'free'. I found myself on an awful rollercoaster (I hate them!) using all my strength of mind to hold on and stay calm.

So why didn't I just get off? Gosh, a simple question at last! *When we love, we are not free.* We cannot just walk away or stop loving, however uncomfortable things are. One goes on trying – and believing – to the end of the road. Maybe this was the measure of how far I had come in six years… it seemed much more important to me to try and help Alice feel loved and peaceful, to express the beauty of her own soul. And <u>I</u> was learning about feelings and ways of being that I had never known before, and they were good. It may have been pretty clear that this relationship could not last, but it had not yet run its course.

However, I was weakened by these upsets and did something very unusual for me, something I had long told myself I wouldn't do, which was to consult a clairvoyant. I picked one at random from a page of advertisements and did it by telephone.

S   **29th April 2001: Kathryn described the situation, the personalities and the feelings involved pretty well (though I told her nothing except that there had been 'a break up'), but she couldn't really see how things might be resolved. We had to learn through this and make our own decisions. Possibly true, but not very helpful! On the other hand she was very positive that there would be a different and wonderful relationship ahead for me; she described this woman's character and appearance…**

Meanwhile my personal guidance remained apparently consistent and reassuring, whatever the ups and downs of life on Earth. When I read the I Ching, the commentaries still described **a need for 'gentle perseverance and restraint'** but promised that **'disunion' could be overcome and 'negative influences' could be checked, leading to 'fellowship' and 'enduring union'.** None of these things seemed at all likely and indeed as the year progressed the underlying problems didn't change. I was having to learn about patience and perseverance in a big way, and the message was reinforced during the night…

D   **14th May 2001: I saw myself cultivating a large area of ground and planting several trees.**

The traditional interpretation of this is that it is auspicious for love affairs. But it's also pretty obvious that with this activity one has to be prepared to wait quite a while for results!

D   **16th May 2001: I was driving an ambulance on an urgent call to pick someone up and take them to hospital. As I came to a T-junction there was a delay due to roadworks; a builder's lorry was beside me and someone was directing traffic, telling me to wait for a signal. But I was too impatient and moved off, turning left. Then I wasn't sure where to go and the radio contact with the hospital was unclear so I couldn't hear their instructions. When the reception improved I learned that in fact there were two people to meet and the first was back along the road I'd just come down! I was going the right way but in too much of a hurry so I'd missed the proper instructions.**

Characters and situations in dreams very often represent aspects of oneself that need attention, and I understood that this dream concerned *my own* emotional healing (the ambulance) and the need for reconstruction (roadworks). "Things take time" was the message, along with "accept the higher guidance". Point taken. I may have recognised all that stuff about deeper issues and spiritual growth, but I was pretty fed up with all these problems – I wanted to be happy *now*. I was being reminded that our happiness cannot depend upon others but in the long run is about being at peace within ourselves (which may involve healing old wounds). And if there is an impatient turmoil within, we certainly can't hear the inner guiding voice.

However, it was intriguing that the dream also seemed to offer a specific clue about the future in referring to 'an extra person' to be met; did this relate to the clairvoyant Kathryn's prediction? This was a very weird situation: *I was involved and committed in one relationship (even though it wasn't working very well) while at the same time apparently seeing ahead and beyond it to another.*

I wanted a better understanding of this and in particular of what was meant by 'a signal' – how would I recognise it if I didn't know what the sign was? Sometimes I have been successful in 'programming myself' to dream about a specific matter in order to get more answers. This time it seemed to work:

D   17th **May 2001: The first part of this dream identified Alice's estranged husband and suggested there was an illness. Then I found myself at a public event where I saw a nondescript man discretely performing healings. I realised that he was an angel. Feeling distressed, I searched for him and eventually found him outside; I knelt on the pavement and said "Master, please help me." He told me to sit and immediately I went into a deep altered state of consciousness (like a dream within the dream). He asked if I understood the purpose of what was happening in my spiritual life and whether I wanted to continue with it. I said "Yes". Then in the dream I woke up to a telephone call from him confirming my address! The scene moved to the school art room; Break was ending and Period 4 was ahead. A man named Charles walked through, said there was a fire in the swimming pool, then left to go downstairs. A teacher named Alan arrived to help boys evacuate and then I heard the fire alarm.**

I knew that I had been in contact with an angelic being and that he would help me.

His appearance may have been very ordinary (and definitely without wings) and indeed he seemed a touch impatient and unfriendly, but there it is. My prayer had been heard and 'noted'. Somehow I also knew that Charles was going to become ill, that this would precipitate an important change in the situation, and that I would recognise 'an alarm signal' at the right time. Again there was reference to breaking up and the period of four – and another time of emotional burning.

Alice and I had not seen each other for a while but two days later we met almost by chance.

S　　19th May 2001: On the way to that place I listened to a play in which a phoenix bird was reborn from its own ashes. As I left after our meeting I saw the car … EVE.

S　　21st May 2001: A junk mail envelope bore the slogan "Don't quit now – things are about to get interesting."

S　　22nd May 2001: I borrowed a power jet washer from a colleague. On my way home a van stopped alongside me, its side panel bearing an advertisement for "high pressure water jetting" and the name "Act Now".

S　　24th May 2001: Arriving at a restaurant to celebrate Luke's birthday, I saw A 655 DAN which describes Daniel's faith despite the threats against him.

Later, Alice arrived at the restaurant (I wasn't sure that she would come) and we had a really happy evening; despite our troubles it was clear that we still meant a great deal to each other. All of these signs (and others) were encouraging me to be strong. In June, I again dreamed of **aggressive young people confronting me but then changing their attitude**; I dreamed of **being faced by a locked door but then finding a master key**; I dreamed of **a complete about-turn in the place I lived, of hearing an alarm and rushing to a flat numbered 44**. But I was still in a pretty wrecked emotional state, so the angels stepped in again:

S　　11th June 2001: I listened to another radio play which I'd recorded some weeks before. (I should mention that when I

78

decide to record a play it's on the basis of a very brief synopsis in a listings magazine or on the Internet; I record quite a few, so that when I come to play one I have no idea which one it is or what it's about.) This one concerned a couple having trouble in their relationship and about to break up. The man was in great stress, nearly died, and then experienced an altered state of consciousness in which an angel communicated to him: "The old must die so the new can prosper...don't despair... Think about Eve and what she means...all this is about getting over your previous relationships... You are being given another chance. She loves you, even if she did have to send you away to make up her mind... Angels are everywhere..."

I had to stop driving, so stunned by what seemed like a direct message to me! But there was more. When the play ended and the tape ejected, the radio cut in playing a song about dreams which included the words: "When the stars are in position, all will be revealed." I immediately thought of the Grand Alignment just before I'd met Alice and the one due next April...

My birthday approached. That day and the day before, I had encountered four references to a fairly unusual name but it didn't seem significant except that it was similar to Alice's husband's surname.

S   16th June 2001: Alice gave me a gift on which she had stuck (she says it was just a whim) a small golden horn. Somehow I immediately knew that this was the 'angelic signal' – it was of the type sometimes depicted with Gabriel. Then she told me that her husband had just been diagnosed with a life-threatening illness. It was the 'proof' of my angelic contact one month before.

I hadn't understood the appearance of an 'Alan' in that dream but the same name reappeared in several other dreams over the next few months, always as a figure of authority. Amusingly, when I used that jet washer to clean the stonework in my garden the same name appeared from under several years of dirt (presumably it was the builder's name). **On the same day I saw the car number ...567 DAN which refers to "the writing on the wall"!**

This would only make sense in March of the next year, but that month would also see the fulfilment of another funny connection. In one of the 'Alan' dreams on 1st August, which seemed to predict an ending being reached (it was the end of the school year and things were being cleared up), I also saw **a teacher of Spanish named Ruth leaving my school carrying suitcases**. Searching for a meaning, my mind somehow related this to the 'Spanish roof' in my dream of 5th June 2000! Well, dreams often contain puns but even I thought this was a bit silly. However, several months later I learned that Ruth was in fact pregnant and she subsequently left on maternity leave at the end of the next March, just as my relationship with Alice reached its most critical point, the time of ending. Surely this was time travel again? I had no way of knowing at the time of this dream (in the school holidays) that Ruth was pregnant and she probably didn't even know herself.

The dreams and signs were becoming more and more integrated. And even though I was finding my life so challenging, I seemed to be more and more in touch with 'higher spiritual forces' which guided me and urged me to keep faith. They had some truly astonishing events lined up for me that autumn.

Φ

A lot of dreams had been recorded around this time but I had struggled to understand them except insofar that the often negative symbolism **(being under arrest 'until January', my car stolen, my house burgled)** reflected my state of mind, upset and emotionally rather unstable. I was learning that there are periods in life that simply have to be endured. Equally I knew that there would be change, and several of the dreams kept repeating the number four motif.

D   **26th July 2001: I observed a hard fought school rugby match against a touring side from 'Rhodesia' which surprisingly ended 4 – 4. The country had of course long ago** changed its name so there had to be reason for this; instinctively I read it as a pun on the words "road easier"!

D   27th July 2001: Before sleeping I prayed for guidance on why I seemed to have to undergo so many difficult 'tests'. I dreamed of watching university students in teams of four play a series of intellectual quizzes, and being eliminated until just one pair remained. Yes, the path of emotional understanding and healing, of achieving security, was a difficult one. But this dream had an extra element, one which was starting to occur more and more often now, which was that as I awoke from it I clearly heard a voice (sometimes it would be a song) in my head. This time the 'answer' to my question was: "Your commitment must be total."

This was brought home to me just two days later when Alice gave me a hard time over what she felt was my lack of commitment to her... It seemed I wasn't learning very well.

Now, I normally like to make plans for a summer holiday well in advance but this year had been disrupted; I had hoped to spend the summer with Alice but clearly that wasn't going to happen now and I couldn't decide what to do. Then quite by chance and at short notice I came across a 'New Age Camp' advertised on the Internet. I like camping but had never been to one of this sort and was worried that I wouldn't fit in with the other participants who, I assumed, would be much younger than me and with freer lifestyles. Yet I had a strong feeling that whatever the risk this was important, so I booked it. Then a hugely clear and powerful dream replaced my nerves with anticipation.

D   11th August 2001: I drove with my son along unfamiliar but pleasant country roads looking for a restaurant. Policemen were checking the car park. There was a nice atmosphere inside as we took our table and I ordered something that had to be specially prepared. After waiting quite a while I realised that one had to collect one's own food so I walked past a long queue and asked the chef for my 'special number 17' which he gave me immediately. It was an egg dish and very good.

The dream concerned personal nourishment (the restaurant) and security (police always represent this). Something special was being prepared for me (perhaps eggs suggest a rebirth), though I didn't understand the number 17.

In the event the camp, hidden away along pleasant country roads, was great. As soon as I arrived I knew I was in the right place because an **'angel horn'** was being used to call people together. Yes, it was uncomfortable in many ways but several loving people there helped to loosen my inhibitions and I took part in several powerful healing experiences. The climax came on the 17th! We spent the whole day preparing for a mystical ceremony of 'cleansing' at which I would be honoured as an 'elder' of the group with the task of opening the proceedings. This felt very meaningful to me and as the day unfolded I was aware of being drawn into a deeper state of consciousness. When I walked by the River Dart in the beautiful woods nearby I had a profoundly religious sense of spiritual connection. Then when the ceremony reached its focus in the evening, one of the women in the group arrived and sat down opposite me in the circle. With a joyful shock I recognised immediately the woman at the top of the hill in my archetypal dream of 25th July 2000: the same person, the same dress and the same pose. Surely she was a signpost, to tell me that I was on course and, indeed, had reached the top of my hill? The ceremony, indeed that whole day, was deeply cleansing and I left the camp feeling blessed, healed and far more confident.

It is an extraordinary feeling when 'dreams come true', even if the specific events aren't especially important in themselves. There is just this great reassurance that, however difficult, life is unfolding as it should. There is also a sense of wonder at *the extraordinary power of the human mind to reach into the inner stream of consciousness and know the unknowable.* If only this ability could be refined, perhaps we might avert or at least be better prepared for some of life's terrors. In the middle of September, as I have already mentioned, my dreams of April 1998 and July 2000 also came true – though I couldn't possibly have interpreted the latter as an actual terrorist attack. A few days later, however, and exactly six years after our first meeting, Eve did in a sense 'come back'. She was in a personal crisis, needed support and seemed to want to be friends again; after all, wasn't this exactly what I had longed for and believed in during those dark days of 1998? At first I felt confused. But then I listened to my heart and knew that I had moved on a long way since then and our 'purpose' had been served.

S   **18ᵗʰ September 2001: I did go to visit her. On the way there, a short journey, I saw the car number B…TRU and on the way back home I saw …629 DAN, which refers to Daniel's great faith despite being threatened.**

Here, I had to learn something about **belief.** We cannot know if there is a destiny to our lives, if there is a *particular* path that we should be treading. There are those who say that we have all chosen our lives and their experiences in advance according to the lessons our souls need to learn. But surely even if this is so, in our earthly lives we cannot know it, nor can we ever know with certainty the whole significance and meaning of our experiences and relationships. **All we can do is try to be mindful and honest and live with whole-hearted faith in what we believe to be true, and recognise that this can change as life unfolds.** It can be painful when deeply held beliefs change but this does not mean that we have made a mistake; it means that we are truly human and that we are growing spiritually.

To mark this important turning point in my awareness, I did a very unusual thing which I mention simply because it illustrates the immense power of the unconscious. I decided that on All Hallows' Eve, an ancient religious festival, I would carry out a small private prayer ritual to give thanks for my life and express my belief in what I was learning. The subtext was my commitment now to my relationship with Alice (even though I wasn't sure what it was!) It was very late at night. Precisely as I began my prayer, the telephone rang; I knew who it was and I ignored it. Sure enough, 1471 later confirmed that it had been Eve.

Some more real magic occurred a few days later at the Healing Arts Festival. After I had wandered around for a while I sat down with some coffee. I needed to rest my back; for a couple of months now I had been feeling severe pain due to an old injury. Although this was of course basically physical, I suddenly realised that the bouts of pain were also associated with emotionally painful situations – and that I should try to 'let go' of these. Almost immediately the pain left me.

Buoyed up by this and feeling that I was 'in the right place' again, I decided on impulse to have a clairvoyant reading before I left the Festival. I have already said that I regard most clairvoyants as, shall we say, not spiritually very genuine. Sure enough, the woman I sat with talked vague nonsense although to her credit she then admitted that "there was no connection'" and offered me a refund. Instead, I decided to try again with whoever was next available.

S **4th November 2001: I immediately felt a strong energy around us as I sat with the new psychic. With no prompting whatever she described Alice, her personal situation and the state of our relationship in perfect detail. She was adamant that there was an important purpose in all of this for both of us (she called it "destiny") and that there would be "a breakthrough".**

It was actually a couple of days before I realised just how significant this meeting had been, when I recalled an amusing dream of a few months earlier.

D **16th July 2001: I was staying with my lover in an unfamiliar city, where we heard Shirley Bassey singing over a public address system. It sounded good so we decided to go to see her by the river, where a large number of people were gathering. The atmosphere was happy. We stood on a large bridge and saw Father Christmas standing in the river giving out presents! (It was apparent that these had been prearranged by the recipients' friends.) To my great surprise and delight, my name was called out and he gave me two large envelopes – but I woke up before I could open them!**

I had very little idea what this might mean except that it suggested we were on course (the river) and that happiness lay ahead after a period of effort (the bridge). There *was*, despite my philosophical misgivings, some sort of destiny guiding our lives (the gifts were prearranged). The fact that there were two envelopes puzzled me for a while; I couldn't help thinking that it referred to two different relationships. But I remembered all this now because the superb psychic's name had been Chrissie Shirley! Then I also remembered a small event which I'd noted as odd at the end of September. There had been a routine fire alarm practice at school and I gathered with others near the steps leading to the art room, in front of the swimming pool. Casually, I went over in my mind the angelic contact dream of the previous May which seemed connected to this situation. Next to me was a teacher named Chris and after the drill we were walking into school together when suddenly she fell and hurt herself; this in turn recalled the dream of July 2000, very fresh in my mind after the events of my holiday. More connections…

Maybe the dream and these events were, more simply, pointing me towards Christmas. Since the summer I had been deliberately noting very few 'signs' for fear that I was becoming reliant on them. But sometimes they just refuse to be ignored!

S   **11th December 2001: There had been even more upsets recently and I just didn't know where I was. Last night, I prayed for guidance. The first car I saw today followed me for more than ten minutes: M 106 ARK which suggests "be prepared". I had seen this car before, but nowhere near where I saw it this time.**

S   **15th December: On one journey in the morning I saw … AL, … EVE and … JOY. However unlikely, I knew that if anything this could only mean some renewed contact with Alice. Sure enough, in the afternoon she 'phoned and seemed to want to see me, but had other plans for that evening. An hour later they had fallen through so we went out together. It was a very happy time.**

S   **16th December: M 106 ARK again, this time ten miles from where I'd seen it before.**

It was, after all, a happy Christmas. Alice and I had seen little of each other in the previous months but none of that seemed to matter now. Somehow there was indeed a 'breakthrough' to a more peaceful state of mind and by January my emotional life was released from its 'arrest'.

The year just had one more special and humbling sign to offer, though. A little while before, I had read a book about so-called encounters with angels in which it was stated that finding a white feather in unusual circumstances was a sign of an angel's presence. I had thought this was very silly and resolved that I wouldn't accept such a 'sign' – no, I wanted instead a firework rocket to land near me before I'd believe it! As the last day of 2001 dawned, I thought back over all the extraordinary and wonderful synchronicities I'd experienced, and gave thanks in particular for what seemed like an increasing contact with the 'higher spiritual forces' guiding me.

S   **31ˢᵗ December 2001: Just as the New Year turned, Alice 'phoned me to send her love. I was in the garden. Almost simultaneously, *three* spent rockets landed a few feet away.**

V. *Before Completion*

I have a silly little superstition, dating back to a family joke, that whatever plastic toy I find in the first Christmas cracker I open each year will somehow represent my fortune for the year ahead! Well, in 1999 it had been a ring (relationship?) and in 2000 an airplane (life taking off?). This is not to be taken seriously. On the other hand:

S   **15th December 2001: The toy was a tiny plastic centaur, which seemed a bit enigmatic. But later the same day, the day that Alice had made contact with me again, we went to see the new Harry Potter film in which the hero is threatened but saved by a centaur.**

So the creature seemed to represent protection in times of danger. I had also already worked out that 100 days ahead ('cent-') would be the last week of March, a time which several dreams had suggested would be critical; further, it was the time of my next careers event and just before the next Planetary Alignment. But such thoughts of foreboding were far from my mind just now because everyday life was so much happier.

After months of effort I had finally tracked down my old friend Alan. We had been very close at university but lost touch twenty-five years before due to his lifestyle and travel; he was now in America and we spoke almost exactly one year to the day since my dream of 'reunion'. I had interpreted this as reunion with Alice since they have the same initials, but in fact it was with both of them! Another extraordinary fact was that just a few days before my call he had dreamed about me, seeing me as somehow trapped yet able to bring about a healing – a beautiful symbolism.

And at least for the moment my relationship with Alice was better than it had ever been, close and peaceful. It had been very much an on-off affair especially in the last year, and I suppose many people might find this intolerable. But human beings relate to each other on many different levels - physical, emotional, mental and spiritual – and, as we all know, difficulties at any one level can prevent a relationship developing. This does not mean that our connection is not worthwhile; I believe that what it does mean is that *we have something to learn from each other at those very levels of difficulty.* Given enough love and spiritual ambition, many problems can be overcome as we grow in awareness of ourselves as spiritual beings. Moving beyond the problems of our lives and of our minds to a 'higher state of awareness' is the most wonderful and healing experience, putting those problems into a different perspective. That's where Alice and I were now.

Of course, it doesn't always last. We are very much Earthly beings too and the concerns of this plane keep interfering with our vision. Further, even from a spiritual perspective, one person's path may link with another's for a while but then move away. We cannot know how things will be. In any case, each new state of awareness brings its own new and harder challenges – the exams just don't stop coming! Life and relationships are *so* complicated…But none of this means that we shouldn't go on believing in what seems good, and go on trying to do all we can to bring that goodness into the world.

As usual, I read the I Ching for the year ahead.

IC   1ˢᵗ January 2002: Hexagram 5 is "Waiting" – there were no moving lines. The commentary says that "nourishment comes in its own time", just as rain will fall but we cannot make it do so. We must wait with inner certainty (faith) and uncompromising honesty in order to overcome danger… There is a Fate at work which we cannot interfere with.

This is not suggesting that *all* life is governed by some fixed destiny, but that I was now on a particular course which I could do little about. The implication that it is 'the right course' (for otherwise I should have been advised to change things) did not make this any easier to swallow; it is *so* difficult for me to 'do nothing'. But time and time again on this path I have been receiving the guidance that I "must allow myself to be guided". In contacting the inner stream of consciousness, it seems, we must sometimes simply surrender ourselves to its flow; after all, the river knows where it's going even if we don't. Nonetheless, a month later I tried again to get more clues.

IC   4th February 2002: Hexagram 53 is "Development" in which "things follow their proper course". There were three very descriptive moving lines – a man is unsure of himself yet has an honest approach, but things get out of control and dangerous if he tries to go too far, though eventually "his work is complete" and his path is "heavenly". The result is Hexagram 3, a time of storm and chaos but ultimately new life and release from tension.

Being quite used to things getting out of my control, I didn't find this too worrying at first! Putting both readings together, life seemed to be unfolding as it should. But something was nagging at me: in what sense could completion of one's work be a time of chaos? It made me think back to a disturbing dream at the end of last year, the very night before my reunion with Alice and the arrival of the plastic centaur.

D   15th December 2001: It's the careers event again, but it's happening in an unfamiliar place and I don't have full control over it. There are problems with the visitors, especially an artist. I go out with the woman who's supposed to be in charge to have a drink at a nearby pub, but she becomes upset and I have to leave alone, very anxious, and I can't find the right way back…

I still hadn't connected the two dreams to an *actual* forthcoming school event, thinking that 'careers' represented the general course of my life. In fact I was being told *both* that my life would be turned upside down *and* when it would happen. Two weeks later (and remember this was actually a happy time in the real world) my mind went further.

D   30th December 2001: I was with Alice in a large and beautiful house which I knew to be hers. It was just before the end of term and eight o'clock. I was cheerfully planning a flight but she was annoyed with me and walked away; I followed her to a secret garden, her own private place, where she said "It can't work". Later I arrived at the Russian border –

it seemed threatening and I didn't have the right documents. But an immigration officer (in white!) was friendly to me and said that people would help me. My 'wife' was with me and we felt happy and strong.

The house in a dream represents the person and, yes, I saw Alice as a beautiful spirit; but she just couldn't let me get that close. The end was approaching. Yet even as I sensed this, I was apparently looking ahead again to the period of eight and arrival in a new world. As time passed the dreams became absolutely unequivocal.

D   On January 15th, I got into the wrong car, caused some damage by reversing, then came back to find my own car missing.

D   On January 23rd, I was walking happily with Alice in a city, on a hill and near the bus stop for home; then she went to greet someone she knew and never returned. I searched desperately but couldn't find her, eventually seeing myself back in my office alone and at night, grief-stricken, putting things back on the shelves. Just before I left, someone opened the door – a tall, slim and blonde woman I didn't recognise.

It was astonishing that I was seeing the inevitability of the end, yet also beyond it.

The momentum of the inner stream was building to a tidal wave! Here on the surface, Alice and I had grown close again and it was clear that she was feeling nervous of that. Even *she* dreamed of being in her car but unable to control it (though she was in no danger) and of hearing her `phone ring despite it being switched off – unwanted messages insisting on being heard...

S   17th February 2002: I did some work in her garden, cleaning the paths, digging out brambles, cleaning the pond and so forth. On the way there I saw the car L 875 UKE which is an extract from the parable of the sower: "...some fell among thorns...others on good soil." When the work was done she said it felt like her mind itself was being cleared out and that it was very disturbing!

S   Also that week I spring-cleaned my own garden and house, and washed all the windows 'to let in clear light'.

The mental clarity achieved was terrifying.

D   6th March 2002: I was in charge of two prisoners, tied together at the ankles, a man and a woman. We were at a school, outside a dining room. It was my task, a solemn and formal duty, to release them so that they could go in for a meal. I knelt tearfully to remove the ropes, saying "Please forgive me" to each prisoner. Later, feeling great relief, I went into a different dining area where beautiful food had been specially prepared for me.

This was one of the most emotional dreams I have ever had and its meaning was clear: the right thing for us, for our nourishment, was the breaking of our ties. At such a time, it didn't really help to 'know' that something better lay ahead. Three days later, Alice said that she just couldn't reconcile our relationship with her loyalty to her family. She began to withdraw. The 20th March was Oestre, the pagan festival of spring and the day of the careers event; she came to see me as it closed and we went for a drink in a pub (which of course I recognised from the December dream). We agreed to separate. It was as the I Ching had foretold in February, the "completion of our work". And a time of chaos.

IC   21st March 2002: A question about the relationship yielded the descriptive and uncompromising Hexagram 29, "The Abysmal". Water rushes through a ravine. It cannot be controlled. There is danger. One must just hold on and remain sincere. There were no moving lines to suggest change.

S   Less than a week later, major reconstruction work started on the buildings of the school where I worked. You may recall that in my dreams the school represents relationship.

Φ

I was surprised at the time by my own reaction to this new devastation. Another ending. A path, which I had believed so deeply in and worked so hard for, seemed almost to have come to nothing after all. But most of the time I was quite calm, much more so than four years earlier when Eve had left. Perhaps I was in shock, refusing to accept reality. But I think there were other reasons.

Firstly, a huge amount had happened in this world and in inner worlds over the past few years, and while I had often stumbled nonetheless I had come to recognise that there was a rhythm and a purpose to it all. There may have been many mistakes and misinterpretations, but too many signs, dreams and readings had proved absolutely correct for me to deny that life was somehow unfolding according to a true pattern. The sense of guidance and protection brings a certain feeling of security, of inner peace. And while I knew there was a long way to go, I also knew that I *was* living and relating in a better way than ever before – I *was* being reconstructed.

I was learning that the divine pillars of human life are faith and love. Now was the time for faith.

S   **23rd March 2002: Alice and I met to exchange a few possessions. This should have been very upsetting but in fact I felt quite peaceful. At home that evening I picked out at random a film to watch, recorded weeks earlier. It turned out to be The Prophecy, featuring the Archangel Gabriel (complete with horn), and its theme was the testing of human faith and love.**

Another reason for calmness was that I had very clearly understood by now that *all* our relationships are learning grounds. If we connect closely and lovingly to someone then we may naturally believe and wish that the relationship should continue. But it is not necessarily so. Apart from the interference of other factors (material or psychological, for example), perhaps there simply comes a point where we have learned and achieved all that we can together. It's time to move on to a new school course, or even a new school! This can be a difficult wrench, a fearful time, especially when the connection has been on a spiritual level because **such a connection can never be lost** even though we may go separate ways in our earthly lives. The spiritual is the world of the indivisible and unconditional and it doesn't care two hoots or even one hoot for our petty mind games or transitory circumstances. So while it may be perfectly right for our relationships to change and for us to move on, we can find ourselves still getting drawn back to that other world.

S **13th April 2002: I had spent a week in Devon, in fact writing the first draft of this story so far. Driving home on the motorway I began to feel a strong build-up of psychic energy. I saw two different cars with the number plate B...MAD, which didn't ease my mind. Just as I finally approached home I saw M 540 ARK, which is the same reference that I started this whole account with (although in Mark's Gospel rather than Luke's) – the miracle of healing despite others' disbelief. I just knew that 'something was about to happen'. At about 10.30 p.m. I took some rubbish out to my bin at the front of the house;** *precisely* **as I opened the door, I saw Alice's car driving slowly past. She had been out with friends, felt upset, and 'something' made her drive past my house on the way home off her normal route. She hadn't intended to stop and had I not come outside at that moment there would have been no meeting. She came in for a while and some of our pain was healed through our conversation.**

The forces that connect people can be very powerful and, to some extent, beyond our control. This can cause problems for one's new life and for new relationships! It certainly did for me and for some time to come. And there *were* of course times, being human and simply feeling the pain of loss and of loneliness, when all the so-called spiritual learning seemed a lot more trouble than it was worth.

At such times, you cannot imagine how much I longed for an end to all this, an end to the signs and dreams, an end to all the lessons so that I could just have a normal life. But having entered upon this path it cannot be abandoned. Having awakened consciousness of the soul, it cannot be ignored. The door cannot be closed. To do so would be to deny one's Self.

And somehow the Self always knows what we need. In February I had decided (why?) to do a repeat Reiki healing course, a renewal of my awareness perhaps. Or maybe I sensed that I was going to need it, just as I seemed to have done in 1998. Acting on instinct, I picked out a particular course from a page of advertisements even though I rather took exception to the teacher's self-publicity; I just knew it was the right course, and wrote off for information about dates and venues. That same night there were three linked dreams.

D   25th February 2002:
(1) **I cleared out a pond of much silt and overgrowth, then found 'something valuable' at the bottom.**
(2) **I was revisiting Warsaw having been there a few years before, and being driven through the city in a large white car by a guide who knew exactly where to go. When I expected to take a right turn he went left, saying that the journey was easier by train and only two stops. Then I was in a building waiting for a lift apparently with the woman I'd seen in the dream of January 23rd. We went up two floors; I was supporting her because she didn't feel strong, and the muzak was 'Sexual Healing'!**
(3) **We watched a six-a-side football game. My son had a pain in his head and I thought he needed to see a specialist.**

Well, I had cleared Alice's pond a week before but nonetheless the dream seemed to me symbolic of healing, of cleansing the view of the spirit (the pond water). Certainly I was being guided in the right way, carried along, perhaps taking an unexpected turn, perhaps repeating something, receiving a 'train-ing' that would lead to improvement (the lift) and healing. A period of two seemed significant. This healing would also be for *me* (my son). Intuitively, I thought that the football match suggested 'a weekend' and a time period of six; but I didn't understand Warsaw at all.

The next available course turned out to be over a weekend in six weeks time (the <u>6</u>th April), just two weeks after the break-up. It was to take place in a room hired at a Polish cultural centre. The room was on the second floor next to the lift. The teacher's name was, of course, Allan. Note once again how many factual details may be dreamed in advance, when there is *no way* that they could have been known at the time of the dream.

S   **6th April 2002: On the first day of the course I parked my car next to a van advertising "Mark's Decorating" with a `phone number. Reading this number as a reference in Mark's Gospel describes the healing of Legion (almost my name in reverse!). Next day, two cars right outside the centre had registrations M 935 ARK (transfiguration) and G 59 DAN (the writing on the wall – remember the name Alan on my garden stonework and the similar car number that day?). As I left the centre on the last day, the car JON 15 pulled in front of me: "the light shines on in the darkness…"**

Well, at least I knew I had been in the right place! True, I did have difficulty with some of Allan's presentation but nonetheless he was undoubtedly a powerful and sensitive healer and the training left me feeling much stronger, liberated to a great extent from past traumas.

Great movements were also afoot elsewhere as the major planets once more now started to come into alignment just as they had a few weeks before meeting Alice. Another realignment now seemed entirely appropriate. My life quietened almost to the point of standstill. I was tired of the pain and effort, impatient for clarity, and there were many days of sadness when I almost lost any sense of purpose.

In dark nights one does doubt one's own sanity. Wasn't all this guidance just an expression of my own desires after all?

Yet I'm sure it would have been far worse but for the healing course. And however feeble I might have felt at times, *something* was very insistently trying to tell me something I needed to know…

D   **15th April 2002: This was the day after my unexpected meeting with Alice and I had been praying for healing of our situation. I dreamed that I was about to take part in a school six-a-side football tournament; I got changed and ran out carrying a corner flag. The pitch was a large rectangle divided into two by a centre line, with six flags around it. A boy was explaining the arrangements, reassuring me that I (and someone else with me – I don't know who) would definitely participate.**

The football theme seemed to echo the dream in February which had been about the healing course, again the number six being cleared 'flagged up' and repeated. In the back of my mind, however, I also somehow linked it with the dream in December 1999 about two football pitches side by side – but I wasn't sure why. The meaning wasn't clear except that the dream referred to 'change' and there was some reassurance about my future with 'someone'! But I was obviously missing something that my mind was determined I should know, because three nights later I awoke in the early hours, sweating and with heart pounding from another dream with extraordinary similarities.

D   **18th April 2002: I was definitely in the room where the healing course had taken place but now it was almost filled by a large snooker table, marked out like the earlier football pitch and with of course six pockets. I was playing with Alex 'Hurricane' Higgins and 'someone else', a woman, was sitting nearby. Alex fouled the pink, giving me six points. For my turn I had to move around the table to a position directly opposite my initial position, aiming to hit the pink into the middle pocket. But I couldn't see clearly because there was a bright light in my eyes, so the curtains on the far side of the room were closed for me. Then, strangely, more curtains were brought out from underneath the carpet in a corner of the** room where they had been 'hidden'. I was joking with Alex that I would have to get married in order to take this shot...

The room suggested the healing theme again and perhaps Al- referred to the healer Allan. (Oddly, just a few days later I saw a television programme about Alex Higgins.) But I was being told that there was something which I wasn't 'seeing clearly'; I had to 'change my position' completely and there had to be a 'closure'. The most striking feature of the dream was the emphasis again on the number six, and the similarity of the table to the football pitch; again I connected it to the earlier dream which had clearly described an overall period of eight years for this path. *It would be another eighteen months, as the eighth year ended, before I finally understood the meaning of these numbers.*

There were other enigmatic details in this dream though: who was the woman waiting nearby, what was this reference to marriage, and just what was it that was hidden?

S   **On several occasions around this time, the car E 898 LUC seemed determined to draw itself to my attention! On a whim, I took a different route home one day and got stuck in traffic with this car ahead of me. Another time, it approached from the opposite direction then made a u-turn right in front of me and stayed there for eight miles; it then turned off but reappeared in front of me a couple of miles further on. The Bible passage explains the parable of the sower and says that 'hidden things will come to light'. When this car had turned off it had immediately been 'replaced' in front of me by ...115 JOB, which asserts that "God speaks" to us.**

The clue kept being repeated.

D   **24th April 2002: England are playing in the World Cup and 'about to make a change'. I'm wondering who is available and say insistently to someone "Tell me when the exams are over".**

Again, there had to be a 'change' and, if I had understood other signs, the period of testing would be over in 2003. More immediately, however, England were indeed due to play in the World Cup in early June just as my school's exams ended...

D   20ᵗʰ May 2002: I changed my clothes for a size 'one sixth'. Then I was in my garden, walking along a network of paths and through an archway, hearing the word "sixth" again. The dream moved to a school lunchtime when I was offered a delicious dessert by a friendly serving lady; I took it to my parents' bedroom to eat, then went back for more – there seemed little food left but 'something special' was found for me. Finally I was walking across the school playground alongside a colleague named Alan; I had been asleep but it didn't matter because I was now 'free'.

'Change' and 'six' would be essential to my path. Special nourishment would be offered on the way ahead (my parents' room suggesting a new relationship), where there would be healing and freedom. It was impossible not to relate this to that terrible dream in March of the prisoners' release being followed by a beautiful meal.

Yes, I think I knew even at the time what all of this insistent information meant. My relationship with Alice – which began on the <u>fifth</u> anniversary of this path and which was also the fifth important relationship in my life – was indeed over. It had to be closed and I had to change in order to move forward to the final stages of this learning. But however 'beautiful' and 'nourishing' the 'secret destiny' that might lie ahead, we were both finding it very hard to 'move forward'. The same strange inner force that had drawn us together that night in April just wouldn't let us break apart completely: she hurt her leg and asked me for healing; we went to a show which I had arranged months before for her birthday; we went to art exhibitions... and all the time I was aware of the deep connection we had made with each other even though I knew that our paths in life were now diverging. As the weeks passed since our separation, the sense of loss and grief remained almost unbearable. It was a mistake to go on like this but both of us seemed powerless to help it.

This was the hardest lesson I had faced so far – learning to let go of the past. I turned again to the I Ching for guidance.

IC 5th **May 2002: A question about the future course of the relationship yielded Hexagram 17 which concerns "Following", not in the sense of unintelligent sheep but rather the way in which the human spirit can pursue beliefs and ideals, sometimes unrealistically but also often to great achievements. The first moving line of the reading described the nobility of holding fast against all the odds to a belief in that which is "beautiful and good". The second moving line seemed to be a prediction: an eternal union is formed between a follower and an evolved spirit, who has withdrawn but then 'returns'. The result is Hexagram 21, "Biting Through" – an energetic clearing away of obstacles and an application of 'natural law'.**

This question, of biting through the ties that hold us to the past and prevent us from truly growing, is surely one of the most difficult problems for many of us. Often it is because we feel very wounded by painful circumstances, or by some injustice or by what we perceive as others' mistreatment of us. This can go right back to our earliest years and to family relationships and events that seem to have 'marked us for life' at a deep level; then we are especially sensitive to more injustice and mistreatment as we get older, in our close relationships or perhaps in our careers. The difficulty is no less when the wound is caused by the loss of something or someone that brought us joy.

But if we carry this pain around with us in our minds – whether it be anger, hatred, resentment or grief – it becomes a dense cloud that obscures our vision of the beauty of the human spirit and weighs down our steps as we try to move forward. It infects our entire outlook on life. We can become jaundiced or cynical, sad or fatalistic. And however much we try to go on, we find that we are attracting to ourselves the very same difficulties over and over again.

As I described at the outset of this story, I had dealt with my own pain (like many others, I think) by building walls. *The trouble with walls, of course, is that while they may protect us from the potential invading pain outside, they also keep our own spirit shut away inside.* We cannot express ourselves fully. We cannot grow freely. Imagine that you are a medieval king who has built himself a castle complete with ramparts and moat to keep out the enemy. You may feel safe (though beware, no castle has ever proved impregnable). You may feel strong. But as the challengers gather beyond the walls, you can't go anywhere. You're stuck inside. What sort of life is that?

What I had found myself being taught these last seven years was twofold. Firstly, if we wish truly to experience what it is to be human and to access the deepest levels of consciousness that our spirits long for, then **we must tear down the walls**. We must take the risk of being knocked about and bruised by life's demands and challenges in order to know what is beyond them. This is hard. This hurts. It can be like scrambling up the rocky paths of a steep mountain, slipping back on gravel, cutting the hands on sharp edges, sometimes holding on for dear life, sometimes not even being able to see the path... But I had also discovered that there are signposts along the way and sometimes the hand of grace to help us through a tough patch. And best of all, sometimes we reach a ridge or a plateau where the mists clear and there is the most incredible sense of peace and achievement. In the relationships I have described there were moments of deep joy and connectedness to the world beyond anything I had thought possible before.

This only makes the second lesson even harder, for even these moments of revelation and Being must sooner or later be left behind if we are committed to resuming the path. Whatever our 'level of development', the task is only made more difficult if we are carrying heavy 'baggage' from the lower slopes, from the past.

We must let go of loss and anger and fear, of whatever holds us back.

It's easy to say isn't it?! In my experience, at least, this lesson is harder than the first. People say that in order to move on from some trauma we must forgive those who have wronged us. Perhaps sometimes it is also a matter of having to forgive ourselves, for our own weakness or neediness. Personally, I have always had a big problem with the concept of forgiveness – surely there has to be some justice, some putting things right, some recognition of what has happened and an expression of sorrow? (Interestingly, in ancient China at the time that the I Ching was being developed, the highest form of legal justice in criminal cases was compassion for the criminal, who would be released if genuine shame were expressed.)

I've never been sure whether human beings can ever totally forgive. But what I was being taught through my experience now was that we *can* release ourselves and others from the debilitating pain of a situation. If we can see every situation as a learning experience, an opportunity for us to grow as human beings, then the people with whom we are involved are no less than our teachers. And teachers deserve our respect and thanks! This applies to *all* of them, even if they don't seem very good at the job... who are we to judge? And all lessons sooner or later come to a natural end (though they may return at a higher level later) – thus we are free to move on to the next one.

Equally, while trying to think well of others and blessing them for their contribution to our lives, we must try to be gentle with ourselves. Most of us are very much on the nursery slopes of the spiritual mountain. Do you remember how hard it was to get to grips with the quadratic equation at school? Yet that is pretty much the mathematical equivalent of infancy! How much harder is it for us as spirits to learn stuff like unconditional love and forgiveness? Of course we will make mistakes and stumble through our tests and exercises. But the student has only one responsibility (though it is an absolute one) and that is to want to learn, thus to go on trying.

And is the mistake of trying too hard to be loving not better, at least, than the mistake of not trying?

I think this is what the profound I Ching reading of the 5th May was telling me. Yes, I had to try to cut these ties. But the first and most important lesson of this relationship had been the experience and recognition of that which is "beautiful and good", and a determination to pursue this in every moment and every situation of life. But there was a bonus. The reading also offered a prediction that, given such perseverance, there would be a wonderful spiritual turning-point, a 'return'...

As I have said before, consulting the I Ching sometimes feels like being in the presence of a wise and loving Master. Sometimes the signs I describe seem to come from a higher intelligence. I shall probably never know the truth of this. But once in a while along this path one comes into contact with the most powerful spiritual force, which is not only humbling but which actually makes a real and significant difference to one's life.

Nigel Peace

Miracles do happen.

VI. *Miracles*

At about the same time as the sad events of March were unfolding, I received in the post the brochure for that year's Mind Body Spirit Festival to be held as usual in London at the end of May. I had visited the festival many times over the years and it didn't hold the same appeal now as it once had. However, I decided that it would be important to go this time. There was certainly a need for healing; the healer Allan would probably be there, and Chrissie Shirley too. Perhaps the event might mark the start of the transformation that so many dreams had seemed to refer to. After all, the only day I could go would be the 1st June (day one of the sixth month, or 'one sixth'!). It seemed to be the right decision:

S　24th May 2002: The car number M 86 ARK refers to the miracle of feeding the 4,000; this version is different to all the others of the New Testament, in the size of the crowd and the statement that *seven* loaves were used.

S　28th May: The number M 32 ARK only seems to refer to "the Sabbath". Normally I would have disregarded this, except that the next Sabbath (Saturday) would be just *seven* days after the previous sighting, and the day of the MBS Festival.

S　1st June: On my way to the festival I saw M 643 ARK, which refers to the *same* miracle as the sighting of a week ago but is a different account of it (here there are 5,000 people). Then just before I arrived I saw the car M 124 ARK, by now a well-known passage urging me to "be prepared".

There was a good atmosphere at the festival that day. I got myself some healing at one of the stalls and went to an inspiring talk about 'living without fear'. But the most significant moments of the day were still to come. As I have said, I was still upset about the separation from Alice and confused because the relationship, at some level, still existed. It was hard to accept, however well I understood it, that we had taught each other all that we could and that it was time to move on. In a sense, perhaps this is the most troublesome thing for one's normal life about the spiritual path: once one has opened one's heart to love, that love exists and can never go away, however much the relationship which brought it about may change. As I have said, at least making mistakes with this is better than not loving at all. We can only keep trying to do the right thing.

The dream of 17th May 2001 in which I appeared to contact an evolved spirit had seemed to take place at a festival rather like this one, and now that spirit was represented for me by the healer Allan, who was present. However awkward his manner (and the dream spirit had been pretty offhand too), I knew very well that he had a powerful ability. So I had decided to humble myself today and had written him a letter asking for healing in our situation, as if to actualise the dream; giving it to him was, for me, a statement of my faith.

I went home feeling much more calm and went out into my quiet garden in the early evening sun.

S　　**Half way down the path I found a champagne cork. To this day I have no idea at all how it got there.**

This felt like some kind of sign of 'congratulation' that I was going the right way, albeit pretty blindly! This was reinforced about two weeks later when, having read my letter, Allan invited me for a consultation. Just as in that earlier dream, I found myself rising into a very strange and distant, otherworldly level of consciousness as soon as I entered his room. He talked in language I completely understood about paths and mountains and the tasks of the soul, and emphasised the greatest lesson of all to be that of learning how to love unconditionally. He told me, as if 'master to pupil', that I was doing all right but that a cycle had ended and I now needed to rest. It took a long time to come down to earth after this experience, but I felt peaceful and strong for the first time in months. More importantly, it was the first time that anyone had really seemed to understand what I had been trying to do with my life and had said "well done"!

At times, Alice and I were still good friends during this month, though she was just as unsure as I was. But we were about to be presented with a final clarification. By the end of June, many dreams seemed to have been fulfilled: the exams and the World Cup were over, the MBS festival had come and gone, my son's team played at Highgate (the dream of July 2001 – that night I had also again dreamed of my car being stolen) and during the school's next fire alarm practice I stood next to and then walked across the playground with a teacher named Allan (the dream of May 2002). Then the conflict with Alice's family resurfaced (just as her mother turned 88!) and I was again marginalized. This had to be the decisive point. Her path was for her to choose, and everyone must be allowed that absolute right and freedom. So it was time for *me* to let go, to withdraw, to accept. I wrote a goodbye letter. The same day:

S **4th July 2002: As a joke, I had hung a large plastic spider (actually a toy for my cat) from a branch of a tree in my garden soon after meeting Alice two years earlier. The spider in some way represented our relationship. Today, it disappeared from the tree.**

D **5th July: In a city (perhaps Wolverhampton where I grew up) there was a big advertising campaign by an organisation which was promising "to make dreams come true". I was excited by this and got my girlfriend to come with me to see the promotion, encouraging her because she was reluctant at first. We went into a big store called "Evans". There were lots of happy people, all being given a small plate of things including eggs – several of these had been thrown about and broken. We weren't sure where to go but then got on an escalator and went up very fast. At the top we took a shower and were very happy. Finally, two large tickets were given to us to take part in the event.**

Exactly at a very critical and sad moment, I was again experiencing a powerful and vivid dream (the first memorable dream for nearly two months) that seemed to promise not only recovery but a wonderful future in which, no less, 'dreams would come true'.

Nigel Peace

Was it a message from 'eaven?! Broken eggs, of course, suggest omelettes – nothing worthwhile can be achieved without some pain and disruption, and my whole path had been about breaking things down in order to rebuild. The escalator is, like ascending stairs, an archetypal symbol for great and rapid improvement; a shower is cleansing and refreshment; tickets represent opportunity.

But who was the girlfriend? This is something, I now realise, that I often made mistakes with by allowing my desires to interfere with the deeper meaning of a dream (and the same might be said of I Ching readings). At this particular moment, of course, my mind was involved with Alice and the first impulse was to identify the woman in the dream with her. But how could I be seeing a 'rapid improvement' when we were in the very throes of parting again? This illustrates one of the most difficult aspects of dream interpretation. The unconscious mind must naturally use situations and people that are familiar to us in presenting information (or perhaps it is the conscious mind that colours the information with familiarity); we must try to discern the *underlying* information, to detach it from our present feelings. This is very hard to do for ourselves – an argument for sharing dreams with trusted friends or therapists! It took a long time for me to understand (or accept) that while a particular person in a dream may sometimes simply be themself, more often than not they represent an aspect of the dreamer's life. My 'girlfriend' may have looked like Alice but I was dreaming about my own emotional recovery which lay ahead beyond the breakages. As it would turn out, in fact I was again seeing well into the future and the same symbols would reappear in fifteen months time.

Φ

If we are very self-aware, or plain lucky, it may be possible to recognise the defining moments of our lives when they occur. There can be an inner sense of awe, a heightened perception of the significance of everyday events, and there is definitely fear. We generally become afraid whenever something familiar is ending because it means that something different and unknown lies ahead. Even if the familiar past has been uncomfortable or painful, it can be hard to let go of what we have got used to and even invested much effort in. One's career or one's marriage may be deeply dissatisfying, for example, but it can still be very difficult indeed to make changes. Many people feel they cannot take the risk of stepping forward into new territory, the unclear and misty future. We may lose what we have. What we have is better than, perhaps, nothing.

Students may be nervous about the approach of important exams but often there is an even greater fear afterwards. Where to now? Yet it is possible to understand such fear not as a negative emotion but almost as a joyful sign that we are growing, becoming more, learning what it is to be human. If we can recognise that and *risk ourselves*, the defining moment can become a personal transformation, a door through which we pass and need never return to. Thus we embrace our spiritual nature more fully in all that we do and are.

In letting go of that which no longer serves us, we become stronger.

No, we don't get instant peace – fear and confusion reign for a while – but we may be blessed with powerful signs and events which confirm our new path.

This is what happened for me now. Certainly, during several weeks of this early summer, I felt dreadfully afraid. The rollercoaster of emotional life had picked up greater speed and was making the craziest turns through the joy of love and the pain of rejection. I really hate rollercoasters. And there seemed a real chance that this one would kill me if I didn't get off. It is a beautiful thing to touch another person deeply, to feel the peace of unconditional and indivisible love. But human beings – ordinary ones at least – cannot live perpetually at this level of consciousness. We have to deal with the demands of the everyday world where events are constantly moving and where psychological and emotional stresses inhibit the spirit.

In the depths of our being we may be untroubled, but on the surface the weather is whipping up waves. The challenge of peace is to bring more of this deeper quality of consciousness into our lives –

but it is so hard when we are thrashing about in disturbed waters! Of course, thrashing about fearfully doesn't help our chances of survival much…

When I had written that letter, and then the spider had disappeared from my garden, I felt terrified. Surely I was about to drown. This was the defining moment. And with some primeval instinct I knew exactly that what was being demanded of me was that **I let go**. In order to survive – no, it was more than that, it was in order that I could become my Self – I had to stop fighting and just surrender.

Maybe this seems perverse. Is it not human nature, when in difficulties, to *do* something? When faced with problems, do we not try to solve them? That's what I had always done until 1995. And perhaps this is so for many everyday situations. But here we are talking about extraordinary times, when we stand before the door of transformation, caught in the student's snag of having to learn an entirely new way of doing things. At such a time we need a teacher: it may be another human being, a spirit or an angel, or it may be our own inner, wiser consciousness – who knows? The point is that we have to accept our own limitations and simply *trust* in the learning process.

The universe responds.

I had experienced this when setting out on the path in 1995, having to find a new home quickly for myself and my son. I had never owned a house and knew next to nothing about the processes involving estate agents, solicitors and mortgages (except that others told me how fraught with stress it all was). I had very little money and there were complications concerning my eligibility for housing schemes that might help me. So I just set the wheels in motion with some letters, telephone calls and by walking in off the street to the first estate agency I felt drawn to. Then I prayed for guidance, sat back and waited (because I didn't know what else to do). I stopped worrying and let go. As if by magic I seemed to make contact at just the right time with just the right people, helpful and caring and prepared to bend a few rules, and things fell into place; within weeks we had a peaceful and secure new home.

But the challenge seven years later was altogether of a different order. Learning to surrender meant two things. First, there was Alice. I had broken down some mental barriers and stepped through some emotional doors and begun to experience spiritual life. Now I had to let go completely of the very relationship which had given me this gift, to say goodbye to this wonderful teacher who had shared my path. This did not mean losing what we had learned together for that would always be carried forward with us. (It is the most dreadful thing when people later turn against those they have loved and deny the experiences they have shared, because of the pain of parting.) What it meant was that I had to let go of *any and every expectation* I might have harboured for the relationship, and overcome my own fears of loneliness or of abandonment or of my human desires and needs being forever unfulfilled. After all, unconditional love means asking for nothing in return. I found this excruciatingly hard – when love is so rare in the world, how cruel is life that it may not be expressed? – and I admit that I didn't deal very well with it for some time to come.

The other sense in which I was being asked to let go was nothing less than surrendering control of my own life. It was the same lesson underlying every experience on this path so far, but it kept coming back harder and more insistent. Suppose for a moment that there is a God: then right now He was saying "You've chosen this unknown journey and asked for guidance, so stop trying to lead the way". Well, it's one thing to ask for guidance but quite another actually to receive and act on it! But at moments of transformation that is exactly what we have to do: give up and listen calmly. When we are in troubled waters and calling for help, there comes a point when we must stop struggling or the lifeguard will not be able to get hold of us and carry us to safety.

On the spiritual journey, the lifeguard is the river itself. It knows where it's going. It will support us because it is our very Self. So we must surrender to its flow and trust it.

In the summer of 2002 I still wasn't very good at that. The first thing I tried to do was ask the river where it was going. Well, actually I asked the I Ching.

IC   **5th July 2002: "What is God's will for me in the year ahead?" Hexagram 45 is "Gathering Together", describing a time in which people come together in family or community** groups, a time of approach and greatness. The one moving line was at the same time both enigmatic and straightforward: there are secret forces at work bringing together those who belong together. One should simply let it happen, do nothing...

Again it was being suggested to me that I must simply surrender to the inner stream ('secret force'), that there was a destination to my journey, apparently another important meeting. But the result of this reading was **Hexagram 47, "Oppression, or Exhaustion", a time of adversity requiring strength of spirit and inner stability.** It didn't seem logical that a spiritual coming together should lead to such difficulty. But someone was certainly telling me something important.

S   Later the same day I went to the gym where the only available locker in the changing room was number '44'. When I left, outside was the car ...444 DAN which refers to interpreting the king's dream. This was the day after the 'Dreams Come True' promotion. Moreover there were further nods to my intuition about two time periods of four years, the fulfilment of which was now one year hence.

IC   7th July 2002: I tried again, to clarify the previous reading, and the book indulged me with a detailed description of how the path was unfolding. Hexagram 12 is "Standstill" and concerns a period of confusion and disorder, but also shows how this can change if one remains faithful and strong. There were four moving lines, each referring to a new stage of growth. At first there is nothing one can do to influence matters, so one must withdraw and persevere quietly; this standstill will change but one must let it happen naturally – allow spiritual forces to act. So far the reading is absolutely consistent with the previous one (and with that of January, "Waiting"). Then there will be a transition to good fortune but it is still a time of danger for one is not yet secure and caution is needed – this expands on the last reading's result (and clarifies the February reading of "Development" leading to

"Difficulty At The Beginning".) But now I was given a bonus, for the final line looked a little further ahead again to when "standstill ends"; personal effort would still be required to maintain peace, but the result would be "Return", a new cycle in which the darkness is over and people are in harmony.

Happy though the prognosis was, it seemed a long way off (indeed, this reading looked forward more than a year and a half); and the very fact that so much guidance over a long period of time was so consistent (which suggests that it can be trusted) actually did little to cheer me. After all, I was now at 'standstill' and being advised to 'do nothing'!

Φ

Little did I know that I was on the edge of probably the most miraculous of all my mystical experiences so far. I said earlier that if one can surrender then the universe responds. It did so now in the most dramatic and yet very personal way.

S   7th July 2002: on the day of the last I Ching reading I saw again M 118 ARK – "prepare" for something. This sign has never failed to deliver. I now recalled the other recent car numbers suggesting that "something hidden will come to light".

The school year was now over. It felt like pretty much everything was over. I desperately wanted to get away on holiday, to rest in new surroundings where the sunshine might clear away my mental shadows. But when I started checking ferry prices I was upset to realise that I possibly couldn't even afford to cross the Channel with my tent. And then, unaccountably, my very reliable car developed 'an electrical fault' which defied two different garages. Clearly, I wasn't going anywhere: even if the car got fixed, the repairs would probably use up what money I had. At first I was angry and frustrated, but then I found myself accepting that somehow this was meant to be – after all, I've had some experience with the interventions of fate...

S   **12ᵗʰ July 2002: I returned home from another fruitless garage visit to find that a piece of paper had blown off the street onto my front doorstep, with a white feather next to it. The paper turned out to be a flyer, several months old, for a Spiritualist church a couple of miles away.**

I have already described my scepticism about the common belief that white feathers indicate an angelic presence. But especially in the light of the recent car registration signs, I could hardly ignore a synchronicity like this. I hadn't known about this church before and indeed hadn't visited any Spiritualist church for some thirty years, but I knew that I had to go to this one.

S   **18ᵗʰ July 2002: As I left my house to do so, I found that another piece of paper had landed on my doorstep. It was a page from a child's school diary, about seven months old and very weathered. On it was written that a Commendation had been awarded for "good work in History" and also for "team work".**

My spirits were certainly lifted – this seemed like a sign that I had got something right at last! An hour and a half later, however, I returned home utterly deflated by a dreadful evening of vague pseudo-clairvoyance which reminded me why I had left Spiritualism in the first place.

S   **But on the way home I noted the registration M 314 ARK which refers to healing and 'the Sabbath'.**

For a couple of hours I felt pretty stupid for having believed in all this stuff. Then I calmed down and thought it through. For one thing, this whole path has been about having faith – in other people and in spiritual guidance – however irrational it might seem. For another thing, there had just been too many coherent psychic messages lately for all of this to mean nothing. So I resolved to give the church one more try – after all, the next meeting would be on 'the Sabbath'.

S   **21st July 2002: while out in the morning I saw M 370 ARK, referring to one of Christ's miracles.**

S   **Oil painting is one of my hobbies. This afternoon I felt an irresistible impulse to work on one of my paintings, called "Grace". In the evening I arrived at the church to learn that the medium's name was Grace (and the first person she spoke to later was also named Grace). The medium was wearing an unusual t-shirt, which was identical to mine.**

It was a small but pleasant church room occupying the ground floor of a converted private house, and the people were welcoming but not fussy. There was a sparse congregation of about fifteen; I sat unobtrusively towards the back, aware of a peaceful atmosphere quite different to that of three days earlier. At such a meeting there will normally be a few hymns and prayers, much like at any other religious service; the medium will give a short address on a subject of his or her own choosing and then spend twenty minutes or so giving 'messages from the spirit world'.

As this evening progressed I gradually felt a deeper sense of awareness and, unmistakably, I felt the real presence of my father next to me. I should say that we did not have a good relationship when he was alive; although he provided well for his family, he was a withdrawn and remote figure in my childhood, very conservative in his attitudes and, on the rare occasions when we did converse, he could be quite dismissive of my more liberal or alternative interests. To be perfectly honest, though I am not proud to say it, I had been quite glad when he died to be free at last of his shadow. In the nearly ten years since, however, I had continued to feel much pain over this relationship – angry at what I saw as his lack of guidance for me as I grew up, while also sad that we had never had a proper male relationship. Much of this difficult emotion came back to me now in that church.

S   **"I need to speak to the man at the back with his eyes closed," said Grace. "Your father is with you. He wants to tell you that he is proud of you. You had a very hard time four years ago, but you've come through it well and grown as a**

result. He says he is sorry that he never said things like this to you when he was alive." Grace went on to make several other 'evidential' remarks about my family (including facts about my maternal grandfather which were unknown to me but which I later checked and found to be true) and about my personal circumstances; there was even a reference to this writing.

This message was both wonderful and deeply reassuring for me, not only offering encouragement and commendation but it was also an important gesture of reconciliation. It seemed significant that he referred to my crisis of <u>four</u> years earlier (after Eve had left) rather than to my present trouble: surely this would have been mentioned if the medium had 'simply' been picking up information about me telepathically? Indeed, Grace Kennedy was probably the best medium I had ever encountered (and I've met a lot); she was clear and direct in her remarks, asked no questions, gave specific details such as names and dates, and everyone she spoke to that evening seemed to understand and verify what she said. If what she does is mind-reading then that is in itself quite incredible.

For what it's worth, I later realised that this event occurred just two months (one sixth of a year) after my dream in May which described change and healing associated with the number one-sixth.

And probably the most wonderful aspect of the experience was that I did feel *an immediate and genuine healing* of all that inner pain concerning my father and my early life. It is true that he had never told me that he was proud of me and never once said "sorry" to me when he was alive. Now all of that was just wiped away. The effect has lasted undiminished in me ever since and indeed led to a wider healing of relationships within my family. Whatever the truth of the source, this is *real*. It was a genuine moment of grace.

So what of the source? Those who question the reality of spirit contact (and I have been one of them) will have to turn instead to telepathy or clairvoyance, and that of the highest order. If Grace were tapping into some collective unconscious or universal field of memory, and brilliantly so, then this raises huge implications for the nature of the human mind. But when one considers the whole sequence of synchronicities in their totality – from the strange car fault which prevented me from going away, to signs about "that which is hidden coming to light", "God speaks", "be prepared" and references to miracles and the Sabbath, to the flyer (for a church I didn't know about) with its white feather, to the diary reference to commendation and history, the painting entitled Grace, the medium's name and even her t-shirt, let alone the accuracy and appropriateness of her words…well, it's very difficult not to think that these events must have been deliberately orchestrated by some intelligent force or beings. This is a truly mind-boggling thought: it's one thing to suggest that significant ideas could have been introduced to my *mind* (happening to notice certain car numbers, working on that painting or choosing to wear that t-shirt), but quite another to imagine how *physical events in the real world and beyond my influence* (like the flyer, the diary and car fault) could have been created.

The sequence of events was by no means over either – the car was still causing a worrying problem! Didn't this now deserve to be healed too?

S   **31ˢᵗ July 2002: The familiar number M 106 ARK suggested again that I should "be prepared". It was soon followed by ACT 18 … which reads "You will receive power…"**

S   **2ⁿᵈ August 2002: The unusual number LL 51 UKE refers to a passage just before the miracle of the fishes.**

Three days later I took my car to the manufacturer's main UK service centre. They reported at first that they'd never seen this fault before, didn't understand it and would have to refer to the company's design engineers abroad. But then, acting on an intuition, one of the engineers discovered that the onboard computer was giving false readouts; he had to hack into it but managed to reset it correctly, discovering that the original actual problem was indeed a very minor one. It was fixed in minutes, and cheaply!

S   **5ᵗʰ August 2002: Just as I left the garage I saw the registration … RWP (my father's initials) followed soon after by … DAD.**

You can understand, I'm sure, why I felt an overwhelming sense of my father's real involvement in my life at this time. Of course, it also raised questions such as "Why now?" so many years after his death, and "Why not when I really needed him before?" not to mention "How on earth does this happen?" – frankly, I think these questions are just unanswerable until we know, if we ever can, the truth about survival of death. Yet there was even more to come.

My mother was spending a few days with me just now, not an easy visit but our relationship was also now improving. On my way to collect her, a strange thing had happened (though I'm hesitating to call it a 'sign'): I turned on the car radio to hear the name "George" spoken and at exactly the same instant a stone came flying horizontally through my open window narrowly missing me. (I assume that a child at the side of the road had thrown it.) I couldn't help but think at this moment of my friend George Stone who had died not long before; but if this was spirit contact it was pretty unorthodox not to mention downright dangerous (though not, I have to say, out of keeping with George's personality)! Then, on the afternoon of the day that my car had been mended, my mother and I went into the garden to enjoy the fine weather. To encourage her hobby of writing, I suggested that we each write five story titles on pieces of paper, pick one of them at random from a hat and both write a short story with that title.

S **She chose a piece of paper. I absolutely *knew* that she would choose the one on which I had written the title 'Stones'. Then as I moved my chair next to the hedge to begin writing, I saw a small white feather just near my head.**

There was spirit everywhere around me now. Whatever that means. I knew that I had to follow these events up and try to discover more about their significance, so I arranged a private reading with Grace (who, incidentally, lived some distance from London and only visited that church perhaps once a year).

S **7th August 2002: This meeting lasted just over half an hour, and I recorded it. Grace asked only four questions and made more than eighty statements about my family, career,** relationships and personal development – only two were wrong, while five or six were predictions. The detail and accuracy of most of what she said was astonishing, giving names, ages, personal descriptions and medical conditions accurately (including facts about my paternal grandfather whom I had never known but which were proved true when I did some family tree research more than a year later). The 'spirit message' to me was again one of great encouragement and reassurance, with a significant prediction of "renewed love" in the spring of the next year. Meanwhile, I just had to "let go" of Alice (who was also named).

I visited the London church only two or three more times that summer, and to give thanks rather than to seek any further 'messages' (which was just as well since nearly every medium I saw was quite awful). I was determined that this was not going to become a regular part of my life or of my thinking. Despite everything that had happened, I still felt some scepticism (as to the origin of the events) and believed it important to maintain that. Yet the spirit world wasn't finished with me.

S   13th September 2002: M 935 ARK refers to "...my beloved son".

S   17th September 2002: M 106 ARK (again) refers to "...be prepared" and to "I send my messenger".

S   19th September 2002: M 935 ARK again, and also ... NRP (my initials).

S   22nd September 2002: I had a feeling that I should go to the church again today, and was reassured when the first hymn sung was "Breathe in me..." (these words are part of my daily prayer) and the second was "Amazing Grace"! However, there was a different medium this evening, whom I shall not name because she was quite dreadful: she spoke in clichés, was unprepared and rambling, and her 'messages' to others were brief and insultingly trivial. So I just closed down and meditated quietly by myself at the back.

Almost at the end of the service she spoke to me and it was as if her whole personality had changed – now she was vibrant and clear, giving a detailed and accurate description of my maternal grandmother (who had died nineteen years before). She repeated the message of encouragement and congratulation that my father had given, and said that the next year would see much change and improvement; the important time (as Grace had also suggested) would be in March 2003, "when the daffodils bloom". As she finished, the medium described my grandmother holding out a birthday cake with candles on it.

This meant nothing to me at the time, but my mother later confirmed that today had in fact been my grandmother's birthday. Her favourite flowers had been daffodils. And her surname (look again at the car number of five days earlier) was Messenger.

VII. *Give Up, Let Go, Move On*

How difficult am I to guide? Despite the coherence of a whole stream of signs and dreams and readings, and despite the massive reassurance of spiritual messages, I still felt unsure of myself and not a little afraid. Part of the problem was my own scepticism, not allowing myself to accept the most obvious explanation – the reality of human survival and of angelic guidance – which gives many others such comfort. There was no *proof*. And however phenomenal the events, my mind might still have been creating them for itself. Or I *might* yet be mad.

The other part of the problem was that, in emotionally stressful times, one does rather tend to lose sight of the point of it all. Yes, I had learned a great deal, was more in touch with my inner self, was relating in a more caring and thoughtful way with others, and I was more mindful of the sacredness of daily life. Many areas of life (home, family, career) were calmer and more progressive than for a long time. But I wasn't very *happy*. I had broken down many emotional barriers and experienced great love – which *did* bring a certain level of inner peace - but I had not yet learned to accept the necessity of moving on from those who had taught me. I had not yet fully realised that one's peace does not reside in another person, any more than it lies in the future ("I will be happy when…") or in the past ("If only I could go back to when…").

The spiritual path is, ultimately, a lone one. It is a journey of <u>Self</u>-discovery. It is not comfortable. This is not to say that we cannot share our lives joyfully with others, but that we cannot *depend* on others for our own realisation. I was just beginning to sense perhaps the greatest irony of human life:

**In order to know that state of perfect and
unconditional love
in which we are joined with all others at the
deepest level of experience,
we must give up all expectations in
relationships with others.**

119

I had touched that perfect awareness – an experience of 'bliss' - for a few moments once before, the night before Eve had left me. It had just come over me, how and from where I have no idea. Perhaps the fact that she then left should have taught me that it had little or nothing to do with her, or rather that it did not depend on her! I had known great joy with Alice too, and now she was gone. Hey, come on you guys up there, I'm just a man...

This is the *actual* difficulty, I found, of trying to live a spiritual life: there are periods when one feels *really uncomfortable* living from day to day in the ordinary material world. The stream of experiences I have been describing had brought an awareness of 'other worlds', of other levels of consciousness and in particular of a pervasive beauty and peacefulness beyond the surface of our normal physical and psychological life. It's tempting to want to stay there. But we cannot do this – there is a living to earn, people to care for, housework and shopping to do, everyday anxieties and tiredness to deal with... And surely this is how it *should* be. We have to be *involved in it all* while also trying to be decent people if our lives are to have real meaning. What would be the virtue of trying to escape from or transcend normal life? This would be to deny that it had any purpose.

Yet once we have touched the divinity of inner self, there is also a painful ache of *separation* to deal with. The healer Allan had described this well during our talk. Once we have consciously realised our spiritual nature and evolutionary path, he said, we become aware of "how far we are from our divine loving Source". This can make it difficult to relate to others and to the down-to-earth concerns that others find important. We can become prey to the feelings of sadness, fear and bewilderment that a stranger feels in a foreign land. Spiritual synchronicities and inner mental events can sometimes be the only signposts to show us that we are travelling on the right road.

Well, at least in that respect I feel blessed.

S   **15th August 2002: While visiting my friend George's widow, I came across some new major roadworks on the A41 and immediately recognised several physical details from a dream I had noted (but not understood) on 1st October 2001.**

Another odd thing was that, in the dream, I had separated from a travelling companion, had to pay a toll to enter my new road and had received £1.71 change. The only place I found to park my car today was next to two others which *both* had registrations … 171. I sat in my car now and calculated that 171 days after the dream was the day in March when I had separated from Alice. Good grief, I'm even doing maths in my sleep now…

This extraordinary summer ended with a week's holiday in a wooden cabin on the edge of Dartmoor. I went there to be at peace and to write (a story and some music). In that beautiful wilderness I could briefly relinquish the everyday world and feel close to the Source; and towards the end of the week there was a short but powerful and clear dream.

D   **29th August 2002: I was working in a very big, brand new department store, helping to prepare for its opening. It was full of high quality and beautiful goods. The doors were to be opened soon, at eight o'clock.**

So my mind was again reassuring me that all the 'work' I was doing was worthwhile. I was again recognising the period of eight (looking forward to next summer) and a new beginning.

Φ

It was difficult to go back to work and settle into a normal routine in September. I had to get 'grounded' and move on, and life provided just that opportunity within a couple of weeks when I attended an educational seminar and met Cathy. There was a clear attraction between us and we had a lot in common, not least both being at rather crucial times in our emotional lives. Instinctively, I realised that this friendship was simply meant to help us both stabilise ourselves – and there's nothing wrong with that. A dream of six weeks earlier now made greater sense.

D   **3rd August 2002: I was driving fast through country lanes somewhere abroad and realised I was on the wrong side of the road, but managed to avoid an oncoming car and switch to the right side. In a village, I went into a shop to buy chocolates. It was nearly closing time and I found that I had a lot of change in my purse. There seemed to be no chocolate left but the friendly and helpful shopkeeper went into another room and returned with two sorts to offer me. One was attractively wrapped but contained pork, so as a vegetarian I rejected it; but the other box also looked good so I took that.**

This told me that I had to make a decisive move on my journey and get 'back on track'; I knew that this meant leaving the past behind, going into 'new country'. In this case I was going to need and look for some comfort (chocolate!), which would enable me to 'change'. I would be helped and would receive what I needed. The right choice was to leave behind what was no longer suitable for me. Perhaps also the rejected choice represented Eve (who is Jewish, suggested by the reference to pork), recalling the situation of some four years ago when I needed to go forward and it was Dawn and I who had helped each other to recover from personal crises.

So Cathy was my chocolate, and although the relationship developed fairly haltingly over the next month or so, and was never deep, we were good for each other. I was learning to move on. Mind you, as so often before, just as things seemed to be starting to go well again, I started receiving warnings about the ending!

S   **15th September 2002: On the way to the seminar where I met Cathy, I had seen …957 LUC which refers to the disciples setting out on their mission. "If you are not received, shake the dust from your feet…" This seemed very odd, being the very day when I *was* apparently being 'received'.**

S   **9th October 2002: Driving on the way to meet Cathy, I scraped a kerb and lost a hubcap. Don't ask how, but I *knew* this was a warning of being wounded on this journey. A little later I saw …555 JON which reads "Take up your bed and**

walk..." The passage is about healing but I read it as saying "Walk away".

D   22nd October 2002: I went into a local shop asking about 'domestic insurance' but I was told that no such thing is available. Then I had to exchange my clothes and went to a back room; the door was open and a woman said "Mind the cat!" But a cat ran into the room, where there were several birds on the carpet... We managed to get the cat out and no harm was done.

Clearly, this meant that although I was seeking emotional security ('insurance') at the moment, it was not to be found in the present relationship. Again there will be 'change' and perhaps trouble – someone putting the cat among the pigeons! – but all will be well in the end. Next day I did in fact go shopping and recognised the very place I had dreamed about.

S   23rd October 2002: As I left the shop I saw two cars together whose numbers were ... CAT (i.e. Cathy?) and H ... ELL (trouble!)

The message was unrelenting as over the next two nights I dreamed again twice of **wearing inappropriate clothes,** of trying to teach **disruptive children** and **arriving late for school** due to circumstances beyond my control. Next day another car, **L 915 UCE,** referred to the same passage as above: "Shake the dust..." I thought that perhaps I'd better ask the book's opinion of all this.

IC   27th October 2002: Hexagram 54 is "The Marrying Maiden" and obviously concerns loving relationships. The moving line this time described one partner being disappointed by the other, leading to Hexagram 51, "The Arousing" – a shock, a manifestation of God...

S   28th October 2002: Next day a badly driven van forced me to stop my car just as another car with number M 270 ARK

passed nearby: the reference is to paralysis healed by faith and to God's forgiveness.

This was all too reminiscent of the mental events I had experienced during my relationship with Dawn, warning me that it would not last and that I was in danger of being hurt if I attached too much importance to it.

Yet while the present friendship did not become very serious, it did offer many happy and comforting moments that helped to bring me back to 'the real world'. I am grateful to Cathy (as I am to Dawn). But *her* mind was becoming disturbed now, unsure of her loyalties (concerning a previous relationship), and she started to become more distant.

S **14ᵗʰ November 2002: I went to see her but found it very difficult to park so had to drive around for a while in unfamiliar streets. At length I found a space, next to the car B 4 END! Then I noticed that my trip meter read 200.3 and I recognised at once that previous 'messages' were being re-emphasised: the present relationship was about to end and I should look forward to March next year.**

S **15ᵗʰ November 2002: Next day I noted M 688 ARK, the same passage as before about "If you are not received..." but in a different Gospel.**

The relationship limped on towards its inevitable end. (It is relevant to note, I think, that notwithstanding the signs I am describing now I actually experienced less than half the number of omens, dreams and readings during the second half of this year compared with earlier periods in this account.)

I tried to support Cathy but there was nothing I could do in the face of truth.

S **14ᵗʰ December 2002: At the exact moment that "Kathy's Song" started playing on my car radio, I saw M 121 ARK which can be read either as a reference to 'being prepared' or to a 'husband'.**

S   **15th December 2002: H … ELL followed by … 363 LUC which refers to "the salvation of God".**

S   **17th December 2002: At exactly the same place where I had lost my hubcap in October, I spotted another at the side of the road; it was a different design to mine but intact (so I could use it to replace mine) and it had <u>eight</u>-point symmetry. As I retrieved it, a car with number plate … NOW passed.**

So this was at last the decisive moment. Three days later I saw Cathy for the last time. All the signs of the last three months – not being received, paralysis, trouble - made sense. The dreams about insecurity and inappropriate situations made sense. The I Ching reading about disappointment and the shocking manifestation of God certainly made sense.

Cathy was pregnant – by her 'previous' boyfriend.

Φ

It was as if the universe – or the bit of it concerned with me – breathed a huge sigh of relief at this point and said "Now we can get on with the really important stuff". Three profound signs from very different sources arrived during December.

S   **7th December 2002: At the MBS Festival in June I had attended a seminar by Rhonda Britten, an inspiring American 'life coach' whose teaching is about how we can learn to live without fear. I was on her mailing list to receive notices, each of which was accompanied by a quotation from her writing. At this crucial new turning point for me, today's message was especially significant in reminding me of my essential path:**

> *"When you can be loving despite your mood, despite your 'evidence' about the world, and your situation in life, that is when you can become completely aligned with your destiny. Nothing can stand in your way and nothing can keep love from finding you."*
> (Living Without Fear, Rhonda Britten – Hodder Mobius, 2001)

I think this is a beautiful insight and it is one to which I have returned many times for inspiration and encouragement. Mind you, the promised 'result' is not instantaneous! And of course that is the whole point: we must not love *in order to be loved in return* for such an attitude is conditional and based upon expectations of others. The Path requires a simple commitment to love *whatever…*

I hope that what this book shows is that when we *try* to do this, we find spiritual guidance and support. As if in confirmation, there was another sign a few days later at the school's Christmas lunch. I have mentioned my superstition about the contents of crackers. It is silly of course, and only started out as a bit of a joke (it's hard to see the deep symbolism, for example, of a crayon or a pink hair band), but maybe the significance I have attached to it causes me to pick up a certain cracker by psychokinesis?

S   **11ᵗʰ December 2002: In my first cracker of the year was a small plastic angel, complete with horn. Later I was given another cracker – this contained a die.**

Then just before Christmas I finished writing a short story, begun in Devon, which incorporated several of my psychic experiences.

S   **23ʳᵈ December 2002: Feeling pleased with myself, I left the house for a walk and found a large white feather on my doorstep.**

I took the angel to be a reassuring sign of guidance - after all, Gabriel is 'the messenger of God' – and the feather… well, my objection to the folklore about this symbol doesn't seem to have made any difference to the powers-that-be.

But then another altogether more disturbing thought occurred to me. Angels are *dead*, aren't they, or at least in an afterlife? And what am I supposed to think about a '<u>die</u>'? My state of mind was not eased by an I Ching reading for the year ahead.

IC   **30ᵗʰ December 2002: Hexagram 30 is "The Clinging (or Fire)". The philosophy of this Commentary is complex and to** do with our dependency upon inner forces; it stresses the need for humility and perseverance. But the third moving line is stark in its simplicity. It describes sunset, the end of the day, when Man understands that life is transitory; he is aware of death. If he remains calm, he can become free. The result is Hexagram 22, "Grace", a time of tranquillity when desire is silenced and struggle ends.

Rather shaken by this further reminder of mortality, I went downstairs and decided to take my mind off things by watching a film recorded from TV a while ago, picking one at random from a pile.

S   It was called 'Fable' and the opening scene showed a coffin (though it turned out that the man inside was alive)! The film concerned prophecy, omens and synchronicities and the main character in it worked for a television station called "8"…

S   I then leafed through the new TV listings magazine and came across Colin Shearman's horoscope for my year ahead: my life would hit a "major turning point" with the solar eclipse of 31st May.

An angel, a die, sunset and death, freedom and the end of struggle, a coffin, prophesy and synchronicity, and an eclipse (a sort of sunset) in the summer just about eight years from setting out on this eight-year path…Pretty clear, huh? So this was it. I had almost fulfilled all I could on my spiritual path and it would soon be time to leave; the end of the eight-year pattern would be… the end.

I can't say that I wasn't fearful, but at the same time I began to feel a kind of inner peace too, a preparedness. If nothing else, I had learned the changefulness of life and become convinced of the eternity of consciousness. So be it.

But hang on… such a pessimistic outlook was not in keeping with all the other earlier signs, dreams and messages especially those about the regeneration of life in the spring. Moreover I just instinctively knew that my work in this world was by no means over yet. In Fable, the man in the coffin was not actually dead! And as if to confirm these thoughts there was immediately another powerful synchronicity.

S   **1ˢᵗ January 2003: Alice had been abroad and I took a gift to leave at her house to welcome her back next day. I noticed that the flat above hers had gone up for sale; somehow this just seemed to remind me of the need to move on. Then on my way home a car stopped with its hazard lights on in front of me at Apex Corner, the very place where our relationship had been predicted in my dream of June 1995. Its registration was …136 ACT. The first few verses of the first chapter of the Book of Acts speak of resurrection, of God's promise and the power of the Spirit.**

This reading is, of course, associated with springtime and Easter. It was as if I was being encouraged to keep faith with all the previous guidance despite, as Rhonda Britten says, my mood and the evidence of the world. To clarify my mind I decided to consult the I Ching again, repeating my question about the year ahead – as I have said, this is not normally a good thing to do but my need was genuine and I prepared for it with an honest heart. After all, this could be a matter of life or death!

IC   **12ᵗʰ January 2003: Hexagram 59 is "Dissolution" and refers to a time, usually associated with the warmth of spring, when divisions between people are dispersed and disunity is overcome – a true 'gathering together' is enabled when barriers that separate us from others are dissolved. Two moving lines emphasised this theme, describing the dissolution of the very self (the ego, one's desires and expectations) as well as of bonds with others. Through this one rises above personal interests, one reaches for selflessness, and although one might "lose what is near" nevertheless one gains even greater achievements. The result of the movement was the difficult Hexagram 44, "Coming To Meet". This can seem ambiguous according to the circumstances: either a "dark influence" enters the scene and is disruptive to the light, or there can be a**

"true and predestined meeting of Heaven and Earth in harmony".

This reading was humbling. On the one hand it not only agreed perfectly with the previous one but also developed it further. On the other, it took the response to a deeper spiritual level suggesting the real culmination of my Path (as I understood it) and of all that I had been trying to do. I felt a real sense of having received wise and loving guidance, reminding me that I had to "let go" – whatever my own hopes or desires or expectations.

It was still all quite frightening, though, on one level. Undeniably there was still talk of death, whatever form that might take: dissolution of self and of bonds with others, and a coming together of Heaven and Earth, can both be read this way. But then a sudden and surprising thought came to me. I have said before that sometimes the actual words of this very strange book can themselves be synchronistic; so perhaps "sunset" and the "meeting of darkness and light" could be suggesting again the time of the annular solar eclipse five months hence and just short of eight years from the outset of the path (and which the horoscope had indicated as a "major turning point" too). Moreover, the structure of both the latter Hexagrams contained an element whose Chinese name is "sun", and the result was a '4+4'. A conjunction of dark and light could also refer to moon and sun; when researching the solar eclipse I discovered that there would also be both lunar and solar eclipses next November, almost exactly at the eighth anniversary of moving into my new home. This may seem like wild speculation but the symbolism is consistent and, after all, great astronomical events had heralded significant turning points before in this account. Going even further, is it possible that the very Hexagram name "Grace" had a double meaning for me, reminding me of the medium's message about renewal in the spring?

There were to be even more strange signs in this short but very intense period.

S   **16th January 2003: A few days after the I Ching reading, I discussed some aspects of it with a close friend over lunch then returned to school where I had to 'cover' a music class for an** absent colleague. **Walking into the Music School I heard the song "Ain't No Sunshine When She's Gone" being played! This seemed like an amusing synchronous reference to solar eclipse and letting go. I hadn't heard this song for a long time – but on my way home later that day I heard it again on the radio.**

S   **23rd January 2003: A week later I met my friend for lunch again and was given a rune reading which she'd done for me concerning the development of my life. It was almost exactly in harmony with the I Ching, with images of fire and the sun, constraint and stillness, partnership and letting go.**

You will read later that all of these signs and prophecies would prove astonishingly accurate in the most dramatic fashion - although I did not die!

Meanwhile, however, there was more work to do, more growth to achieve. I have a friend who is an experienced psychotherapist and over a long period of time we had discussed the value of 'regression therapy' as a means of understanding at a deep level how difficult experiences in the past might limit our ability to grow and to live freely in the present. Perhaps the process might help one to release emotional blocks or get past unconscious fears that hold us back? I had some misgivings about it, especially about those therapists who claim to access 'past lives' and to interpret our present challenges in terms of traumatic experience in previous incarnations. This seems to me a prejudicial approach, one that imposes an unsubstantiated set of beliefs (to do with reincarnation) on the process – how can one trust the interpretation of the outcome if it depends upon something that is simply unknowable? But my friend assured me that to her mind too this was not an essential part of the process, so I agreed to try the therapy.

For one reason or another the opportunity hadn't arisen before, but now 'by chance' it did (at exactly the right time for me) and my friend was able to arrange it for me. In the event all kinds of things went wrong on the day. It turned out that the therapist chosen was not only a 'past lifer' after all but was also disorganised and neither very professional nor very experienced. Mistakes were

130

made. The process was very difficult for me. But I believed that I had been guided to undertake this so allowed it to go ahead. At one point the session was interrupted and I decided to take a break outside (this was in a town I had never visited before, some distance from home).

S　**3rd January 2003: Immediately I went out, I saw two separate cars with registration ... PAX nearby. The word means 'peace' in Latin, and of course it is my own surname. Somehow I felt the presence of my father reassuring me that the day was an important step forward.**

The rest of the session was again difficult and I eventually left the place feeling pretty battered, raw with the exposure of several deep and painful emotional wounds – it was a nightmare journey home. But by extreme good fortune, the friend who had set it all up happened to be visiting London that day; she telephoned soon after I got back and immediately came over to look after me. And quite perversely the process did seem to work after all! Within days I could feel that 'something had broken', some barrier had been removed and a healing, a new calmness, was beginning. The past difficult experiences themselves weren't of course removed and nor had the pain of them evaporated; but it was as if I had now been freed to move on to a new level of being wherein they were no longer relevant. It was rather like the spontaneous healing of my relationship with my father that I had experienced the previous summer.

And so, when I met Alice later in the month, we found that we were able to move on. This extraordinary month (and the Chinese year!) ended with one more beautiful guiding sign to remind me of the previous year's breakthrough and its promise for the future.

S　**29th January 2003: I received a letter from my mother enclosing a very old photograph which she had "just come across". It was of my grandmother. She was holding a birthday cake.**

Φ

One day the next month I happened to meet Alice again quite by chance.

S   **17ᵗʰ February 2003: At that very moment a car passed by with the number M 404 ARK. This refers to the parable of the sower and specifically where it is said that "some seed fell by the wayside".**

This Bible story, beyond its normally accepted meaning, is an inspiring reminder to us individually of the necessity for faith and perseverance in trying to live good lives. Many things we try to do or achieve or become will just not 'work out', while sometimes we'll have a little success for a while. We must accept this as the nature of life, just as some seeds fail to grow at all while others take root but then wither. But we must never, *never* give up for sooner or later the seeds we sow will find fertile soil and yield wonderful fruit. We find that *we* have grown. Nature itself is extraordinarily determined after all – have we not all been amazed to see plants growing up through a concrete pavement? Life finds a way.

So it was that despite the foreboding omens of January and the sense of separation in February, there were now also signs of renewal and hopefulness all around. There was the early spring colour of snowdrops, crocuses, primula and daffodils in the garden, while the first buds were appearing on the rose bushes. The major renovation work at my school (which represents relationships in my dreams) was nearing completion. Then a **huge** dream – the first I had remembered for three months – seemed to confirm that life was as it should be.

D   **5ᵗʰ February 2003: A school term had ended and a new one was about to begin, at New Year. Someone was driving me home but then stopped the car because they could go no further; with some difficulty I got myself into the driving seat and took control. We were about to cross a border.**

We arrived outside a tall building in World's End (a district of London) where a group of teachers challenged me to get to the top of the building; there were just over one hundred steps and it had never been done before. I was teased by a

happy, tall, blonde woman who ran ahead of me fast – it was hard to keep going but we made it to the top. There was a great sense of inspiration and achievement.

As we began to descend, the scene changed: it now seemed that we had entered the building to save two small children, a boy and a girl, from a fire. When we reached the street successfully there were many people there congratulating us. I was shown the front page of The Times newspaper where there was a story about me saying that I had been knighted in the New Year Honours List! The story also showed a photograph of school musicians giving a concert in which all the music was by father-and-son composers (this was linked to my having rescued my son). The achievement of one hundred steps was repeated. I felt a great sense of satisfaction and contentment.

As I awoke from the dream I heard the song 'Visionary' by the rock group Strangelove playing in my mind.

This was a strange psychic vision about love! When I woke up I noted that the time was just after ten past four in the morning (that is, about 4.12 a.m.) and immediately made a connection to the dream of 21st January 2001 in which I found a "Good Life" at 4.15 p.m. Naturally, I now did a mathematical calculation and realised that one hundred days into the New Year would be 10th April, or 4.10 – the present dream had featured 'just over one hundred' steps, suggesting perhaps the 12th or 13th of April by this reasoning? The content of both dreams and the very timing of my awakening were consistent: the promise of happy achievement just over two months hence.

But this dream contained *much* more! The first part speaks of the end of a relationship and a letting go of what can no longer work (the car stops at the end of term), and the beginning of a whole new era (new term and New Year) in which I gain greater control of my own life (driving the car across a border). I had lived in World's End more than twenty years before when I was first married; for me it represents change and a new start – after all, an end is also a beginning. Perhaps some might think that the 'teachers' I met there were spirit guides but, as I have said before, perhaps all those with whom we share relationships are our teachers. I understood the dream to be predicting a new relationship, although I didn't recognise the woman!

However, this relationship would be far more than just a happy affair. It would be an experience through which we might both be able to reach 'the inner child' (rescuing the boy and girl from fire) and heal the deep wounds of the past. This would indeed be a wonderful achievement, the most 'honourable' of steps on one's spiritual path. Such a 'rescue' leads to no less than harmony of the soul (in the dream, music). Again I felt the strong influence of my father guiding me (the composers represented in the concert), whether real or psychological.

It was not lost on me, however, that the dream was not predicting happiness-ever-after and an easy ride. No achievement is without effort and rescuing from flames requires great courage and the acceptance of danger, even perhaps injury. But I felt really inspired now, by the unfolding spring and by the powerful dream, and I knew that life was about to take an important turn. No, it was more than that: **I was approaching the climax of all that I had striven for over the last eight years.**

A few more signs reinforced this feeling.

S   6th **February 2003: The very day after the dream, I encountered the car DAN 629 which refers to Daniel being honoured, his faith having been tested.** [4]

S   19th **February 2003: I took the opportunity to upgrade my mobile 'phone to a better model with a stronger battery – my old one had been letting me down frequently lately. Now this may not seem very exciting or significant, but for me it**

---

[4] S   13th November 2003: I have to mention here that more than nine months later I was writing a draft of this book. You will read later how significant this period was. Having written the passage above, I took a break and went outside to discover that some neighbours had a new car that was now parked outside my house. Its registration was S 1 RNP (which of course I read as SIR NP). So I had been knighted after all!

represented 'new energy' and 'better communication'. It would also prove extraordinarily symbolic seven months later.

S   22nd February 2003: Earlier in the month I had met an attractive woman at a party in Oxford and today I went to see her for our first 'date'. We met at a pub just off the A44 – her choice, but of course I couldn't help seeing these numbers as significant. I had taken her a small narcissus plant as a gift and its first yellow flower opened that very morning, recalling my grandmother's message of the previous September.

This is an example of the danger of attaching too much or literal importance to omens. Yes, I couldn't help *thinking* at first that this meeting might be the one that had been predicted. But the truth lies in our *hearts,* and in mine I knew that this relationship was not going to develop. I was being impatient, over-anxious now to move on.

Still, I only had a couple of weeks more to wait before the situation became quite unequivocal!

S   10th March 2003: I was running late and made a sudden decision to change route. I immediately saw, near each other, two cars with registrations ... JOY and M 106 ARK. The latter ("be prepared") has been mentioned before and has never failed to predict an important event.

VIII. *The End of Time*

As soon as I saw Bettina, I knew that we belonged together. She stood with her back to me, wrapped up in a big jacket against the cold wind, twenty yards away on the touchline of a school football match. But across the distance between us I could feel our energies reach out and embrace. Indeed, as I approached I had to deliberately resist the instinct to go forward and put my arms around her! Later, she would tell me that she had felt the same instinct.

I'm no good at all at small talk or smart one-liners and knowing what to say when you're attracted to someone. But this situation was different – somehow we already knew each other very well – so I just went up and said hello and we started talking. In the crowded tearoom after the game, she took the hood of her jacket off and I watched mesmerised from across the room: she was the woman who had run up the steps with me in my dream of five weeks earlier.

She then had to leave and there was no chance to talk further, but that night another powerful dream confirmed what was happening.

D   12th March 2003: **I visited a fair and then went back to visit it again... Now I found myself going on a long and important journey abroad by car with a woman beside me. We approached a major crossroads and just as we had got to the other side I turned to see huge waves of seawater flooding across where we had just been. I said that "We were just in time" and "This is a strange place".**

Later I found myself alone travelling in a foreign country where I saw a sign indicating the South Pole ahead. I entered a small town and stopped to look at a plaque to the side of the road (when I awoke, I couldn't remember what was on it). Some children watched me with interest. Then a large and dangerous spider jumped from its web on the plaque onto my shoulder; I brushed it off but then it jumped on me again and again I had to brush it off.

Nigel Peace

At this time I couldn't understand the first element of the dream except as a pun on the word 'affair' – but why would I go twice? This only made sense much later. The 'long journey abroad' is a fairly obvious archetypal symbol for an important new path in life ('a strange place'), and the 'crossroads' indicated a fundamentally decisive time ('just in time') of great emotional significance (the 'flooding water'). Yes, I knew this.

But there was a stark warning here too. I could be heading for a cold and icy place... and I was going to have to distance myself decisively from Alice (the 'spider'). Again, this would happen *twice*. In fact, I met Alice again the next day for a theatre visit arranged several weeks before.

S   **13th March 2003: I felt ill at ease all evening and when I got home I found a very large spider on my bedroom wall!**

S   **16th March 2003: I decided to clean the windows of my house, inside and out. This was a normal spring-cleaning job, but I was acutely aware also of the symbolic 'clarity of mind' achieved in letting more light into my home. I was rewarded...**

D   **17th March 2003: I was in the Great Hall at my school at the beginning of a new term. Some architectural changes had been made, changing the shape of the place, and I wasn't sure what to make of it. But then I looked up to see that a beautiful new vaulted ceiling had been built too, and now the changes seemed very good to me.**

As I have said, the school represents emotional relationship for me (what I need to learn about most) and the Great Hall is its heart. I was being restructured! During this week Bettina and I talked on the 'phone a couple of times, long and already very friendly conversations although she was also trying to 'hold back', saying that she was in another relationship at the moment. I could *feel* that this wasn't true but in time came to understand her reticence – she had been most dreadfully hurt in the past. Yet neither of us could deny the energy between us; and when I drove to her house for the first time:

138

S 17th **March 2003: I saw two different cars with registration ... JOY as I approached her road.**

Things were happening very fast now and we were indeed in a strange place, already meeting deep feelings and strong hidden fears. Five days later we had lunch together but now there was somehow an undercurrent of tension; we agreed to meet again later for dinner.

S 22nd **March 2003: On the way I saw two cars close together, ... RON (my father's name) and M 679 ARK which refers to Jesus commissioning his disciples and warning them that they may not always "be received" well.**

It was an awful evening of emotional upset when Bettina was clearly very troubled about the issue of letting go of the past – we even bumped into her previous boyfriend in a restaurant! She needed reassurance and a sense of security but (in the interest of honesty) I had been naive enough to tell her quite a bit already about my journey of the last few years. I assumed she would realise by this just how important she was to me. I am very stupid sometimes. We talked for hours at the very edge of risk and trust, and with a depth of understanding I suspect many couples take years to reach – but the forces of fear and pain were also very great.

S 22nd **March 2003: When I got home I discovered a water leak in an almost inaccessible place in my bathroom. Water was running through the kitchen ceiling and I just couldn't stop the flow completely. Already shaken up, I began to feel I was being overwhelmed – in its relatively small way, this was the 'decisive flood' of my dream on the night after we had met!**

This was a perfect example of the synchronicity between ordinary life events and important developments in our inner lives. I knew this was a critical time, and there was much more to come. But next day I had no opportunity to deal with either problem since I was committed to taking a group of boys to an important sports tournament. I patched up the leak as best I could and set off.

S 23rd March 2003: On the way I saw together … TAO (which means 'the spiritual path') and M 387 ARK, another reference to the commissioning of the disciples, who were given the power of healing.

In the middle of the tournament that afternoon, Bettina called me on my mobile `phone to say that we couldn't continue our relationship because she was too afraid that I couldn't let go of my past feelings for others. I can hardly remember ever having felt such desolate emptiness as in that moment. We were both in tears but she was determined. In a flash I remembered a dream of several weeks earlier, before meeting her, that hadn't made sense then.

D 7th February 2003: I was watching the final set of a doubles tennis match, a very close fought thing. It was won by an Indian pair and I found myself calculating an 'average score' which turned out to be 7 – 52. One of the players then showed me exactly the same figures on a calculator.

I had realised that this concerned something decisive, probably to do with relationships ('doubles'). For some reason, 'tennis' often seems to suggest argument in dreams (hitting back and forth?) while – and I have absolutely no idea why – in my own dream experience Indian people always represent difficulties. The numbers were a clear reference to a time period of seven weeks. I realised that we were now into the seventh week since this dream and at the end of that week was Bettina's birthday.

On the way home, however, there seemed a glimmer of hope.

S 23rd March 2003: In close proximity I saw the registrations … CLU and H … ELP and … RWP (my father's initials).

Well, perhaps I *was* clutching at straws, but this made me feel that my father was in some sense present and reassuring me. At this crucial moment in my emotional life I wasn't 'being received' yet there would be a 'healing'. Nonetheless it was a horrible week ahead.

The leak got worse so that I had to call an emergency plumber, with the consequent expense and disruption I'm sure you're familiar with. I had difficulties at work and began to feel exhausted. My car was clamped! Bettina didn't want to talk. Perhaps all these things seem like fairly ordinary worldly events? It is difficult to convey the utter turmoil of my heart and mind just then, mirrored in everyday life. My entire spiritual path of nearly eight years had centred on issues of relationship, learning new ways of being, learning how to love… and I already knew with certainty that Bettina was the most important woman I had ever met. There was simply an undeniable *destiny* between us. This was my greatest ever challenge (perhaps hers too). We had profound things to teach each other. But within two weeks of meeting, all this seemed to be collapsing around us.

How shallow! How faithless! How feeble!

Had I not learned anything from these years? Given that I made a lot of mistakes, surely I knew at least not to give up or run away when life gets difficult. And I knew that I had received an inordinate amount, perhaps more than anyone deserves, of coherent 'guidance' that made sense and showed me the way forward. Yes, living with an open heart means being vulnerable to pain, to being tossed about by life's waves and sometimes being overcome by emotion. So this was the time when I had to reach for a place of inner stillness, to listen for the current of the river beneath its surface, to persevere in belief.

I do not go to church, I do not chant, or meditate for hours at a time. But however bad I feel I start and end each day by lighting a candle and having a few minutes of silent prayer in a special place at home. Sometimes I will also practise Reiki healing. This does not lead to instant clarity but it is a gesture of faith that gives structure to the day and, little by little, helps me to become more mindful in the real world of inner, quieter levels of consciousness. Over time this has brought a measure of calmness concerning what is or is not really important. I also have the blessing of a certain strength gained from the overwhelming evidence of life's purposefulness seen in the spiritual guidance described in this account. There have been so many clear and accurate precognitive dreams, for example; even if I cannot always interpret them fully at the time (since they often involve people or events not yet encountered) their intent is clear and one learns to trust the process (and improve one's interpretation) as their meanings unfold in real events. Likewise, by paying attention to these things one develops a better intuition about the significance of events.

So at the time of great disturbance described above, I reached for the inner place of quiet and strength and asked for renewed guidance. I recalled February's dream of huge promise (which certainly predicted a future for us beyond March!). I found faith. And perhaps even above all of this, I listened to the truth of the love in my heart.

I would need to call upon all of these resources again and in the most desperate circumstances in the months ahead.

S   **30th March 2003: I saw ...835 JOB. "Appeal to God. Be honest and...he will help you now." There is also a reference here to 'learning from the past'.**

Later that day I made a hopeful call to Bettina and we talked for nearly three hours, the longest telephone conversation I have ever had in my life. Next day she invited me over and again there was that beautiful peace between us; we could not hold back now, and kissed for the first time. Somewhere, the universe sighed with relief.

Next week, we both went away on holidays booked before we had met but in every other way we were still totally in contact. She came to meet me on my arrival home and we made love for the first time.

It was the 13th of April, just over one hundred days since the New Year (see the dream of 5th February), just after '4.10', and it was now a very 'Good Life'.

We became very close and happy, talking on the `phone every day, seeing each other several times a week; I could simply not remember any time in my life when I awoke each morning so full of energy and optimism, so sure that I was on the right course. This is not to say, however, that everything was easy! In particular, Bettina was finding the speed of it all difficult to deal with and had very real, justified fears about intimacy and trust. Sometimes it seemed that

142

whatever I tried to do to reassure her was not enough and she would retreat for a little while behind a protective wall. I had already had a presentiment, while on holiday, that this was going to be the most challenging issue for us.

D **11th April 2003: It was a Sunday evening just after six o'clock and I was outside the main gates of my school in a car with 'my family', about to leave on a journey. Then I received a telephone call and someone told me urgently "You must get out *now!*" Immediately, some Special Forces personnel arrived with cables and other equipment to make the place safe.**

I recalled previous occasions when I had had warning dreams just as a relationship was properly beginning. In the context of what had happened two weeks before this dream, I knew exactly what it meant. The 'family journey' was my life ahead with Bettina, protected by 'special forces'... But you will remember that the school had previously represented my relationship with Alice (before it was 'restructured' in the March dream) – I was being warned to be clear about letting go of her completely, for this is what Bettina needed. If I knew this, then I should have also realised that the dream contained a specific prediction that the issue would become critical in six weeks time.

Meanwhile, I *did* heed the dream and was encouraged by further signs.

S **14th April 2003: M 124 ARK ("be prepared") was followed by H ... ERO ("be strong").**

S **15th April 2003: ... 115 JOB refers to 'making sacrifices'.**

The next weekend was Easter, a blessed and terrible festival signifying both death and new life, the triumph of spring over winter, and the true spiritual turning point of the year. This Good Friday was a black day. I went to see Alice, who was still a friend though we had had no contact since the theatre visit in March, to tell her about Bettina and to say a final goodbye. It was incredibly difficult to do, *not* because I had any doubts whatsoever about the new way but because I did still care for her; as I have said, love does not evaporate when life's circumstances change. The relationship had been over for a long time, and I thought we were at peace with that. I certainly wasn't prepared for her reaction of shock and upset. I didn't know how to handle this and I probably seemed quite cruel towards her. She didn't deserve that. Death.

Then on Easter Day Bettina came with me to meet my family, a happy and peaceful day all the more so because my family life had been so troubled in the past. It felt like a true and profound healing was taking place. Resurrection.

One further major event at the end of this month touched me very deeply:

S 28th April 2003: **The major restoration work on my school was finally complete and a small ceremony was held to mark the achievement. It seemed very important to me that I should attend because this whole period had had such symbolic meaning for my own inner life. Minutes before it began, Bettina arrived completely unexpectedly to be with me having taken time off work simply because she understood the significance of the occasion for us. I could hardly believe how much *I* was being loved.**

Φ

It is interesting that, despite all the renewed activity of my personal life, the frequency of dreams, signs and readings remained at the same reduced level of the previous year. In the first twenty-nine weeks of 2003 I had only eight memorable dreams and read the I Ching only six times (an average of around once every four weeks or so). I noted ninety-four car registrations and there were ten other important synchronicities (together an average of one every two days).

You may be thinking that in this account I am only referring to a selection of these that 'made sense' and ignoring many that didn't, but it is not so. Certainly, a few of the dreams and readings were not fully understood (although virtually all were in the course of time) but there is no question of their meaningfulness and coherence. It is more true to say that a higher proportion, about a quarter, of the synchronicities such as car registrations held little or apparently no meaning for me and I think one would expect this to be the case: there are many car numbers that are *potentially* significant but it is unreasonable to expect every observation of them to be so. The moment and the life situation must be taken into account, and it will always be a subjective judgement whether a genuine synchronicity has occurred. In any case, is it not utterly remarkable that *any* of these events should be meaningful?! Finally, I am not of course listing every dream and reading and sign in this account because on the one hand that would be very boring and on the other hand many were concerned with matters (for example friends, career, finances) not relevant to the spiritual theme of the journey I am describing.

Perhaps the real reason for the 'settling down' of these phenomena is simply that I was by now well established along the path and if I often didn't know quite where I was going at least I was confident of my direction. So I didn't feel the need to read the I Ching, for example, and my unconscious mind needed to speak to me less often. This is certainly true of my relationship with Bettina – I may not have known how it would 'work out in the end' but I was totally certain that we belonged together. As you will read shortly, I didn't even consult the I Ching about us until more than two months after our meeting.

It was already apparent, however, that there was great *spiritual purpose* in our relationship. She was undoubtedly the most challenging woman I had ever met, both intellectually very clever and also extraordinarily sensitive, with both tremendous strength in dealing with the world and also a deep vulnerability as a result of life's wounds. (What challenges *she* has to meet in this life!) For me it was a matter of testing and developing further everything that I had tried to learn so far about relating to others more thoughtfully and lovingly.

Most of the time this wasn't at all difficult – I was crazy about her! But as time passed and we became so close, some very difficult situations emerged. Many of these were essentially similar to others I had encountered before; there was a continuation of the pattern. For example, there was family resistance just as there had been with Alice. I recall the dream of 27th February 2001 in which there had been *two* separate 'threats' by young people, as well as the prediction of a meeting with a woman now recognised as Bettina. And she, just like Alice, would sometimes become nervous of our growing intimacy and withdraw (though fighting defiantly) behind security barriers.

As the eighth anniversary of my path approached, all hell broke loose. I had been warned in the April dream but had failed to recognise the predicted timing then. So I was reminded.

S   **7th May 2003: M 124 ARK has been mentioned before and speaks of 'being prepared'.**

S   **13th May 2003: First there was M 270 ARK followed by … SAD and H … ELL.**

D   **15th May 2003: My son was captain of a football team playing a cup final, a very tough and close match. The opposition scored but it was disallowed, then we scored through an accidental own goal. There were now ten minutes to hold out but I knew that our team would win.**

The second car registration above refers to Jewish lawyers objecting to the way Jesus was speaking. Clearly, this was going to lead to big trouble. Hmm, Bettina is Jewish and a lawyer... As for the dream, I confess that I completely disregarded it at first because I had been watching football the previous evening and my own favourite team were indeed soon to play a final. But of course it *is* our everyday thoughts that are often used as the language of important dreams and the unusual features of this one should have alerted me. A goal being disallowed is 'something that shouldn't happen', while an own goal is 'a mistake' – no matter that it was the other team scoring it, for any character in a dream may be representing an aspect of ourselves. My son, therefore, represents me (a spiritual youngster) and I am being urged to play the captain's role, to be decisive and determined.

Just four days later, Bettina's behaviour suddenly changed, becoming defensive and harsh; neither of us really knew why this was happening except that, despite all my reassurance, she felt threatened. Well, I have said that she is sensitive: she was clearly sensing events of a day later when out of the blue Alice contacted me and needed to see me, to say that she was in great pain and sorry for everything…This tore at my heart and I just didn't know how to deal with it properly. It 'shouldn't have happened' – after the warning dream in April I had told her that the parting was final, and I don't know what else I could have done. But I made the mistake of not being clear and decisive enough *now*. This caused Bettina upset and sadness.

I was being asked the most serious questions now. Yes, I had loved Alice but life had taken a new path and there was no doubt in my heart of my commitment to Bettina. On the other hand, she was now rejecting me! Who and what should I trust? The incredible irony of the situation was that it was through my relationship with Alice that I learned to trust my heart, never to give up when all seems lost, to risk everything and to bear pain. It was clearly time for a reading.

IC   **21st May 2003: I asked what was God's will for my relationship with Bettina. By this I was asking about our spiritual purpose together; perhaps we had met purely to challenge each other along the way rather than to form a lasting bond? But Hexagram 32 is "Duration" and concerns enduring union between people, in which one must change with the times while one's inner being remains firm. There were two moving lines both warning that moving too fast or with anxiety will lead to misfortune; true duration can only be created gradually. This was a pretty good description of our relationship thus far. But "misfortune"? The outcome of the reading was one of the most favourable Hexagrams in the whole book, number 14 "Possession In Great Measure", which name almost speaks for itself; it is described as a union of strength and clarity, a graceful powerfulness achieved through dedication to modesty. This too described beautifully the feelings that we had already shared at special moments.**

Despite this accurate and deeply spiritual response, I was still confused and in pain. Bettina was not being at all nice or understanding! We had our first row and a very major one at that. Walking in the school gardens, I prayed despairingly and asked for 'a sign'. I cringe now at my own foolishness, but in a moment of weakness I found myself suggesting to God that a white feather, like last summer, would mean that I was making a mistake with this relationship whereas a black one would mean that I was on the right course...

S   22nd **May 2003: When I went to bed that night I picked up a magazine of stories that had lain untouched since its arrival weeks before. The first story I read described a character being covered from head to foot with black feathers.**

We were in a very strange place, in love but hurting each other, afraid of being together and of being apart. We made up, and if anything our feeling was even deeper than before. But there were still warning signs.

S   6th **June 2003: 629 DAN in which Daniel's faith and belief is tested.**

Then the walls came crashing down again, inadvertently toppled by Alice again. She called to say that her mother, with whom I had been friends and whom I used to visit, was seriously ill. Once more, Bettina felt threatened by the past relationship and wanted me to give up all contact, including with the old lady. The next fortnight was unimaginably horrible as Bettina turned away and I wrestled with morality, while everywhere around me I seemed to see references to the numbers 'eight' and 'four plus four'. It was now my birthday, the eighth anniversary of the decision to leave my marriage, and as I reached the end of this cycle I felt that I had failed completely. I had taken great risks, lived and loved with all my heart, but it seemed that I had lost everything.

S   16th **June 2003: For my birthday, a friend mentioned earlier did a Rune reading for me: "Strength and sacrifice will**

148

bring joy and victory. There are battles ahead but the outcome is good if you do *not* fight." I was being told again to keep faith and trust with humility in the guidance of spirit.

S   17th June 2003: JOB 378 says that "the animals go back inside their dens", meaning that the danger is over. This was followed by ... JOY.

D   18th June 2003: At first I found myself with a group of wild lions, moving among them and reaching into each one's chest to touch the heart. As I did so they became peaceful. Then I was in a chapel, knowing that someone close to me had died. There was a feeling of sadness but of completion too. I arranged several small glass vases of blue flowers on an altar. As I woke up I could hear in my head the Barclay James Harvest song "We Will Survive Beyond The Grave".

There was a clear link between the first part of this dream, the signs of the day before and that of the 6th June. I had to be brave, despite my sense of loss. And, all over again, I had to be very clear about letting go of Alice (the vases were reminiscent of some she owned) once and for all. Figuratively, I had to kill her. Again.

Hearing a song as I wake has been a fairly common experience that has always had a deep impact, reinforcing the message of dreams (as on the 5th of February) or sometimes replacing them. This time I had a strong conviction that it represented my father's presence with me. The feeling stayed, and was very real, for several more days. It urged me to do some very extreme things and even now it rather shocks me that I was capable of them. First, I removed paintings connected with Alice from my walls and then I returned a birthday present she had given me. I threw away her letters. I told her again that there was to be no more contact between us. These things were unimaginably hard because I felt they were immoral and dishonest. I felt ashamed.

But, incredibly, *things immediately started to change.*

S   23rd June 2003: I turned on the car radio and heard a play entitled "My Dad Knows", which was about people sometimes having to do dishonest things for the sake of others. Further along the road I saw two cars, firstly **M 57 ARK** which refers to "breaking the chains" and then … **88 JON** where Jesus says "Let he who is without sin throw the first stone".

So perhaps, I felt, I might be forgiven. That evening I wrote to Bettina telling her what I had done and that I loved her.

S   24ᵗʰ June 2003: I got up in the morning and walked in my garden, to find that the very murky pond water had completely cleared overnight. I have absolutely no idea how this happened. Then I went to deliver the letter and on the way saw 799 DAN which describes God's glory and ultimate victory.

It was the reassurance she needed and she responded immediately and lovingly.

S   25ᵗʰ June 2003: The car … 119 LEV refers (in Leviticus) to "the need to make sacrifices".

S   26ᵗʰ June 2003: M 23 ARK tells of how the paralysed man was healed, while …136 ACT tells of the resurrection and promises the blessing of the Holy Spirit.

IC   3ʳᵈ July 2003: A belated birthday reading for "My year ahead?" yielded the simple response of Hexagram 43, "Breakthrough". It describes a time of release from a long period of tension but counsels that one must still be very aware and resolute in developing one's character.

At the time this seemed wonderfully simple, the signs together almost appearing to suggest that everything would now be fine… Oh no, the spiritual life just isn't like that and I would later discover that the words held a double-edged meaning. After all, if a major cycle was now ending then a new one must be beginning. And when any growth cycle ends and another begins, there is a very critical period of hiatus in between.

For the moment, I couldn't have cared less. However challenging the path, I had absolutely no doubt that we were on course together and the next two months were just extraordinarily happy. This most complex and fantastic of women did not become a soft pussycat overnight and there were still some very difficult days when she felt hurt or afraid. But little by little we were handling these moments better. She began to trust and open up more to me, and there was such a powerful love between us then. My parents' anniversary this year – exactly one year after my first meeting with the medium Grace and my father's healing message – was one of the happiest of my life, as for the first time we spent more than twenty-four hours together and totally at peace. The last day of our first holiday together in August simply *was* the happiest of my life as we touched an unimaginable depth of union.

Perhaps I hadn't failed after all.

IX. *The Fire*

We can never know exactly what are the inner purposes of our experiences. We can never know the full extent of what it is we need to learn in order 'to be all that we can be'. We can never know whether we have 'succeeded' or 'failed' or what still lies ahead to challenge us. We are like small children in a great school, gradually working our way through the levels, the pleasures and the tests, always developing yet always with much, much more to learn. We might reach the relatively senior levels of a school, with some achievements under our belts, but there will always be another more senior college after that where we will start as freshers. Our teachers are also always (hopefully!) at least a few steps ahead of us and showing us the stage to which we can aspire. But even they always have further levels of growth to achieve.

All we can do – if we choose to accept the challenge – is to throw ourselves wholeheartedly into the school experience and accept the knocks as well as the plaudits that come our way, with *trust* in our teachers and *faith* in the educational process. *We just have to keep trying.* And the key to a meaningful life – one that we can be proud to have lived and which makes a difference in the world – is **awareness**: we must notice what goes on and try to fit it into our understanding, and know that it *will* fit in some day even it makes little sense now.

Of course this kind of analogy can be stretched too far! But in my experience of teaching young men, it is not at all necessarily the most talented or those with privileged backgrounds or the most attractive or those who are most at ease socially who are the most 'successful' in the sense of becoming well integrated people best able to recognise and take advantage of the opportunities that life presents. Rather, it is simply those who have *cared* most about doing their best, those who *involve* themselves most in all that the school and life outside it have to offer.

In the summer of 2003, eight years after my deliberate intention to set out on this path of learning, I knew that I had achieved (with the blessing of many others' teaching) something very special. The depth of love and sense of divine union, beyond thought itself, which I experienced with Bettina, was far beyond the imagination of the man who had started out. My gratitude is eternal. The spiritual purposefulness of these eight years was undoubted. *But all the same, I was still only just beginning.*

At that time, driving home so happily from our holiday at the end of August, it would have been impossible to imagine the horror to come. Simply as a man, I felt joyful and believed that this could continue. Don't we all long for that contentment? But just as we can never know what it is we have yet to learn, so we can never know what life will present us with: yes, I have shown that it is possible to see a little way forward and around us, but we cannot know the truly critical turning points. Perhaps this is because, obviously, we do not yet have the experience of them to be able to understand their impact. We may have presentiments, but life-changing moments, whether disastrous or happy, have a natural habit of appearing out of the blue. This is the very nature of human life, when we are thrown back upon naked faith.

> **"Wake up there, for you do not know when the Lord will arrive among you."**
> **(The Gospel of Luke, chapter 12, verse 40.)**

Within a couple of days of that happiest of days I entered the most extraordinarily intense and painful period of my entire life.

Immediately on our return from holiday there developed an inexplicable distance between us. Maybe, having been so hurt in the past, she was now fearful of our very intimacy. Everything seemed to be misinterpreted and gestures of love were dismissed, as the barriers went up and she demanded 'space'. The breakdown of communication spread.

S   **1st September 2003: I had recently bought a new portable radio. It stopped working.**

I had been so looking forward to the new year at school, feeling optimistic and strong, but instead my days were starting with tears. In this very dark state, I read the I Ching for us.

IC   5th September 2003: Hexagram 37 is "Family" and the moving lines described the roles and moral responsibilities of the man (consistent care) and woman (balance) required for family union. The result was Hexagram 49, "Revolution".

S   6th September 2003: Next morning I went out into my garden to find several black feathers by the door (an earlier symbol representing Bettina).

So I prepared myself for testing times and changes in our relationship. But I was still inwardly confident of life's new direction because the love I felt was entirely unchanged. I had no idea how bloody the revolution was to be. But as things developed it was as if a stream of events and signs and dreams presented themselves to warn and protect me.

S   7th September 2003: The Internet service provider Freeserve sent me a free trial horoscope. It warned of "tense moments this week", "harsh words being exchanged" and said that "What you are facing is truly a turning point". (Despite my scepticism of press astrology in general, this particular site proved so astonishingly accurate that from now on I took notice of it.)

D   8th September 2003: That night I had a shocking and powerful dream in which there was an angry breakdown of communication with Bettina. She told me that "It's your baby!" Then I found myself, struggling with luggage, in the foyer of my hotel but unable to open the four-digit combination lock of the door. I could see someone through the glass but they couldn't or wouldn't help me. A woman who had been with Bettina came in and continued to chastise me in French, but I couldn't understand much except that she referred to Bettina as "ton mari". In a while she became calmer and opened the door for me, then left saying that she would return later.

I awoke cold and frightened. The upset was somehow my responsibility ('my baby') and my past experiences ('baggage') was blocking the way ('locked door'); yet I wasn't understanding the situation ('foreign language'). It was odd that despite her anger the woman used the familiar "ton" and the incorrect "mari" which means husband – was this a punning reference to 'marriage'? The only reassurance to be gained from the nightmare was that the door *was* opened and the woman *would* return… I had to search my behaviour and motives, and be strong and patient. Next day, to reassert for myself my commitment, I changed the four-digit PIN on my mobile `phone to a number that represented Bettina. And then:

S   **10th September 2003 : The `phone was stolen from my private office at school (although the pocket tape recorder, which still held the dream account and which was next to the `phone on my desk, was not).**

You may recall that I had seen this new `phone as representing a time of new communication and that I had received it just before meeting Bettina. But the theft meant more than a breakdown; I had a distinct feeling of being under personal psychic attack and, without denying my own responsibility, I knew that some outside agency was threatening our relationship. We had now been together just six months and indeed we spent a happier evening celebrating this, but there were undercurrents…

S   **13th September 2003: I still had my old mobile handset but when I tried to use it found that it was 'security locked'. A new SIM card had been ordered but I couldn't contact Vodaphone to activate it. Similar frustrations and misinformation continued for a full week before this situation was resolved and I was 'back in contact'.**

S   **14th September 2003: Twice this weekend I had unusual trouble with my contact lenses, managing to put both into one eye at one point and then losing one while out driving with Bettina. This was just after seeing, having changed route and** become stuck at a junction, **M 121 ARK** ("be prepared"). When I got home later, I saw several spiders in the house.

From the inner levels of consciousness I was now getting strong hints about what was building up. There was a situation that I wasn't 'seeing clearly' (the lenses) and it was to do with Alice (dream references to my past, reversion to my previous `phone, and the appearance of spiders). I knew that Bettina felt insecure about this but I really had worked hard to reassure her, and there had been no contact since the issue had arisen earlier in the summer.

S   **15th September 2003: Nonetheless, the FS horoscope this week was insistent: "...family issues... emphasised. Expect a blast from the past, or perhaps even the return of an ex-lover." It also promised that emotions would "get churned up"! When I left home today, the car ... 442 JOB pulled in front of me ("your words can heal...") and then I saw a white feather stuck to my rear window.**

In the present context, the feather of course also represented Alice (the rear being in the past). And it was entirely appropriate that next day Bettina and I went to the theatre to see the play 'Power', which is about the changing nature of personal power in relationships.

S   **17th September 2003: BLACK WEDNESDAY.**
On the way to work I saw the unusual registration M1 11GHT followed by ... 115 JOB, which refers to an attack.
Then I was given a rune reading about the current situation by my friend who has been mentioned before. It described "a total blockage" and my partner being "unable to free herself from past troubles"; there is a "path to freedom" but it is also blocked, while I am also unable to be my true self due to the stress of the time.
I turned on my office computer to find an email from Alice. She said that her life had been very hard recently, she was low and just wanted me to talk to her.

The signs of two days before now made perfect sense, but what was I to do? I felt that I couldn't ignore a call for help especially from someone who, yes, I cared about. This was my test, my baby... and the decision that closed and locked the door. I didn't want to be furtive. Our relationships surely mean nothing if we cannot be open and honest, and accept one another completely. I wanted to be open about this event and reassure Bettina that it did not affect my love nor threaten us. Who can ever say whether this was a mistake?

S   17ᵗʰ September 2003: On the way to her house I saw the number ... SAD.

I didn't even get a chance to be reassuring. She was dreadfully upset and sure that I had been betraying her. It was clear to her that I wanted to break us up. What terrible, terrible experiences her soul must have endured before. It was "over". I drove home numb with shock and trembling with fear.

S   17ᵗʰ September 2003: On the way I collected my mobile 'phone, now repaired, and exchanged my portable radio for a new one. Communication restored... For what it's worth, I also realised that today was the eighth anniversary of meeting Eve.

IC   20ᵗʰ September 2003: "What's happening?" yielded Hexagram 43, "Breakthrough", which I had also received as my birthday reading in the summer. An incredibly apt moving line described "a man in an ambiguous situation" who must try to be true to himself despite loneliness and others' misjudgement of him. The result, unaccountably, was Hexagram 58, "The Joyous".

S   21ˢᵗ September 2003: The FS horoscope helpfully pointed out that there could be "all sorts of complications if you aren't aware of what you are doing", and added that I was likely to make a difficult situation even worse!

Yes, there was certainly plenty of complication and misjudgement about now by all three of us in this unsought-for triangle. How could I not be ambiguous? Throughout the eight-year path I had tried to learn to be more honest and loving, but perhaps I was also very naïve – it doesn't always seem to work in the real world. Apparently it is not acceptable to care for more than one person, all others must be totally rejected. *I now felt like a complete stranger on this planet, unable to make out more than the odd word of its foreign language.* It crossed my mind now that perhaps the 'evil' I had done, for example, by turning my back on those I cared for, was being revisited on me.

All I could do now was try to be true to myself, though it was unimaginable how this situation could ever again become 'joyous'. I tried again and again to approach Bettina but she, her friends and family rebuffed me, even though Alice selflessly wrote to reassure her. And the universe wasn't being very helpful now, as continuing signs themselves seemed ambiguous.

S   **23rd September 2003: In one of my maths classes, a boy repeatedly and pedantically made an issue of a particular multiplication sum. I realised that the numbers involved were, exactly, those of my `phone PIN (which I had just reset in the old `phone). Later the same day my office computer developed a fault. The engineer thought it had been interfered with; fixing the problem in my absence he reset my password to a random numerical one – again, Bettina's numbers.**

S   **27th September 2003: I delivered a loving letter and flowers to Bettina hoping to clarify matters, but on the way there saw the numbers ... TAO... WOE and ... NRP (my initials). Sure enough, another negative reply came later.**

IC   **28th September 2003: Had I got it all wrong before? Was my belief unreal? I consulted the book again for my relationship with Bettina, and received Hexagram 26, "The Taming Power Of The Great". This is a time for holding firm when everything depends upon perseverance and self-renewing strength of character so that even the most difficult**

undertakings can succeed. The two moving lines were unbelievably encouraging: harm is prevented, the obstruction is overcome and one's principles prevail, leading to "the way of Heaven". The outcome was again one of the most fortunate possible, Hexagram 34 being "Power Of The Great". This describes union characterised by fluent strength, "in harmony with Heaven".

Such an auspicious response seemed inconceivable given my dark state of mind and the actual evidence of the real world. Could the situation really turn full circle for us? But on the other hand I have mentioned before the danger of interpreting dreams or readings according to our desires; perhaps this reply was more personal to *me* than for *us* – that is, I must continue to persevere in what seems right and thus the present harmful obstruction to *my* path could be overcome...

Access to the unconscious is a wonderful thing but understanding the information is quite another. As September ended I was still in turmoil and at my lowest point for years. I felt reduced virtually to nothing, my efforts having failed, my beliefs broken, my 'guidance' seeming false. I felt close to death.

I had to try to renew my strength and clarity. Symbolically, I bought a more powerful battery for my `phone and cleaned my entire house including the windows. I carried out a personal prayer ritual at Rosh Hashanah, the Jewish New Year, asking for healing and guidance. But a group of Bible references didn't seem to make sense. First someone put up a notice outside my office (advertising a meeting) quoting **Luke, chapter 12, verses 1 – 12 ("...things that are hidden will become known...")** and then in quick succession I saw the cars **629 DAN (the lions' den, faith tested), S ... HOK and ... 41 LEV (where God spoke to Moses).** Within a day of this they certainly were, it definitely was, and He did!

I had recently begun investigating my family tree, so as better to understand my forebears' characters and patterns of behaviour (and thus to know myself better). I now received simultaneously a horrible letter from a family member reflecting several of my own (hopefully now past) most difficult characteristics, and a devastating letter containing previously secret information about, in particular, my father. (Incidentally this research would later make sense of some things that the medium Grace had said months before, about a family member I had known nothing about previously.) The knowledge and awareness I gained through this work was of incalculable help to me in understanding how we go about relationships and deal with personal challenges; it also helped to continue the healing within the family that had begun the previous year. But although for the first time I found that I was able to mourn properly those who had gone before, the process also released a lot of grief at a time when I was not in any case emotionally strong. In a sense, it both strengthened and weakened me. It may have been an important spiritual step forward, but I wasn't sure I could take any more...

Perhaps it was not surprising that at this new depth of inner awareness I should now experience one of my most powerful dreams ever, from which I would awake with an absolutely clear sense of 'a spiritual presence'.

D   3rd October 2003: (The dream was very long and detailed so I have abbreviated it here.) I found myself having to defeat the threats of a powerful vampire along with other lesser demons, which I managed to do but sustained wounds in the process. After a long and difficult journey across a wilderness back to safety, the wounds were healed. But then I couldn't find my car and was refused help by certain figures of authority. However I received a text message guiding me across a large empty car park and out through a gate, where I was told that I was safe. Then I was rescued by a woman in a French car, but only after I had forcibly removed another car blocking the way and my rescuer had driven on a long detour through the empty space that I had crossed. A man sat patiently nearby in another car. I was told that he was 'my Master', and there was an enigmatic reference to marriage in Westminster Abbey.

Nearly every part of this dream except the ending was immediately clear to me, from meeting the personal emotional challenges of my blood family (the vampire and demons) though not receiving the support I needed, to being guided (by texts!) when I lost my way. I was being told, it seemed, that although things would take time and I had to go through some 'emptiness', nonetheless I would be safe. An obstruction had to be removed but then there would be a new relationship. My partner would also have had to go through that emptiness, so I must be patient. The reference to the man in the other car left an inescapable sense that this loving reassurance had indeed come from a spiritual Master. *I felt that I had received a direct and holy response to my prayer.* But why a French car, and what was the significance of Westminster Abbey? I would wrestle with this for months.

S   3rd October 2003: On the way that day I heard a radio play about having faith in Jesus and in healing.

The week continued to be difficult but Bettina and I were in touch and agreed that we were missing each other. Unsurprisingly, I looked forward hopefully to the Jewish Day of Atonement (Yom Kippur), a time for forgiveness and reconciliation.

S   6th October 2003: The weekly horoscope spoke of "a turning point in a relationship" and "a time to change the pattern"; I had to be able to "let go and move on". I talked to Bettina on the `phone later that evening, then turned on the TV just as a character said the words "God has a plan". Well, I wished He would let me in on it…

S   8th October 2003: 42 DAN says that "God shows us signs and wonders" while M 23 ARK describes healing, but soon after this there were two cars with registration H … ELL! The latter has nearly always been followed shortly after by difficult times. It struck me that the reference in Mark included the numbers "one in four" and I wondered if this could represent a time period (as in my dreams): one quarter could mean three months or perhaps three weeks…

S   9th October 2003: One after the other I again saw S … HOK and … 41 LEV where "God speaks". A little later, on the

way to Bettina's house, my driver's side mirror was broken by another car passing too close; surely this means "Don't look back"? Then as I left her house I turned on the radio just as the song "Move On" by Santana was playing.

S   10ᵗʰ October 2003: There were notices up at school quoting the same text that has come to characterise this whole period – Luke, chapter 12, verse 35: "Be ready, the Son of Man is coming when you least expect him."

For more than a month now I had been living every moment of every day in a heightened state of awareness and, yes, of some fear. I could feel the surging waves of the river of consciousness within, in what can only be described as a tide of fate carrying me along. It was a momentous time and a dangerous time and I could do virtually nothing about it. My heart was full of love and entirely open, vulnerable to every knock and rejection. But I knew that Bettina too was in pain. I couldn't turn my back or close my eyes and walk away however much 'God's signs' seemed to urge me.

And just *how* were all these consistent (and ultimately truthful) warning signs being caused? Perhaps I was achieving some strange level of consciousness where we can read the patterns of that inner stream, and so in the world around me I intuitively took notice of those things – such as car numbers – whose meaning resonated with that esoteric awareness (and of course did not notice those that didn't). Even so it is astonishing just *how many* small events could be synchronous (such as the numbers in the maths class and 'random' computer password).

These experiences suggest that everything around us is meaningful. But this still doesn't really explain, for example, how often I seem to turn on a radio or television to hear something absolutely apposite to the moment. I surely cannot have unconscious awareness of every radio or television broadcast, or of every other electromagnetic signal, being made at any one time! (Critics may argue that for every apparently meaningful such moment there are a dozen meaningless ones and I'm just being selective. This is of course true, but quite irrelevant – all that matters is that meaningful synchronicity does sometimes occur.) As I have said before, there have been so many phenomena where the 'simplest explanation' is that of some sort of spirit guidance. This should be borne in mind during the next few pages because something, somewhere, was definitely somehow protecting me.

Meanwhile there was another in what was to become an extraordinary sequence of vivid dreams.

D   **10th October 2003: I was having problems with my computer, similar to what actually happened two weeks earlier, except that now the voice-recognition software (which I don't have) couldn't understand me. I tried all I knew to fix it with some limited success but it still didn't work properly. In particular it was misreading the word "suspicion". I explained the problem to a colleague named Dave who is a computer expert and who might have solved it – but I still wanted to try to do it myself first.**

It was clear enough that I wasn't being understood however hard I tried and indeed that Bettina was 'suspicious', or wary, of my loyalties. Perhaps I needed some professional, expert help? Something was trying to help me, or at least prepare me:

S   **13th October 2003: The weekly horoscope said "you might be knocked off balance" by coming events and have to "cope with more than you bargained for"; there would also be a very difficult conversation. Great! In the morning I saw … CLU just as I turned on the cassette player to find that I'd recorded in error a play about a healing miracle. Later in the day I again saw S … HOK, though a different car and in a different place than before.**

D   **14th October 2003: Against my will I found myself persuaded to enter a drama competition and, very unexpectedly, I won it. Only then did I realise that it was a very prestigious award and would bring great opportunities, including travel to southern Africa, and indeed almost a new career for me. There was also a prize of £20,000. Another dream the same night saw me entering a 'dating competition'**

and being given a ticket which was drawn third! I expected to meet a blonde woman but something interrupted the event and there was a long delay. Later, however, I did meet her and we travelled happily in a bus to the seaside which was twenty minutes away.

Yes, I was certainly and reluctantly involved in a life drama now, though all the evidence was that I wouldn't win it. That very evening Bettina came round and again said that our relationship was over. The conversation lasted three hours and was horribly painful (so the horoscope was spot on there): although she loved me and the relationship was very important, we were "too different" and she didn't trust me. The dream of four days earlier was confirmed while last night's seemed ridiculous. In what sense could all this represent a happy and successful new path in life and winning a 'third dating prize'? And what clue was the repeated number twenty offering me? All I could think of was that twenty days hence would be the anniversary of my father's death.

I felt close to death myself now. I had tried everything I could to be loving and honest and to live spiritually, trying to be mindful of what is good and to care for others despite my own wounds. Of course I still made many mistakes, but as I had set out to do eight years before I *had* changed my way of being and I *had* found the deepest joy. And lost it. The warning signs were all true. The encouraging ones must have just arisen from my own desires and optimism.

It seemed that I had nowhere left to go. I felt myself begin to break into pieces.

Φ

I'm not sure how I survived the next week or so, my job also being very demanding at this time. I woke up each morning longing for unconsciousness and with no idea how to get through the day. The next weekly horoscope urged me to **"let go… to make room for the new"** and warned that I might encounter my **"deepest fears"** and feel that my **"security is threatened"**. Spot on again. Except that I simply could not let go.

IC   20th October 2003: **A question about the future of the relationship yielded Hexagram 19, "Approach". This describes a time of increasing greatness and success, although there could be "misfortune in the eighth month" (and this was indeed now the eighth month since meeting Bettina). But one must "persevere inexhaustibly" and with a great-hearted approach. The result was Hexagram 41, "Decrease", a time when one must be still and draw upon one's inner strength and the power of the heart to compensate for what is lacking in the outer world.**

I couldn't tell from this what sort of future was being indicated. We were certainly in a period of 'decrease' but the commentary speaks of this as a time of spiritual good fortune, while the moving line also urged me to continue to be loving and sincere. And despite my state of mind I again began now to receive reassuring signs…

S   21st October 2003: **After several frustrating delays I finally obtained a replacement mirror glass for my car, and thus 'new vision'. Immediately afterwards I saw JOY … and then, to the rear, T … SAP; reading this in the mirror it suggested that the PAS…T was now behind me! I recalled the sign of 'Move On' when the mirror had been broken.**

S   22nd October 2003: **Again after much delay I tracked down a special battery I needed (new power). Just as I left the shop I saw … 442 JOB: "…Your words have helped others…Now trouble strikes you down and you are afraid. Shouldn't you… trust in God?" This was followed a few minutes later by S … AFE.**

Extraordinary small synchronicities were beginning to tell me that, whatever was happening in the world, I was on course and would be all right. As a result of my work on the family tree I visited some relatives with whom I had had virtually no contact for many years; this proved very revealing and helped further in healing my grief especially concerning my father. But also while I was there my relative had insistently and for no apparent reason shown me **a picture of a dragon** and then a little later produced a large (dead) **dragonfly** from the garden, thinking that this would interest me. Four days later, having just returned from a trip to China, Alice gave me a gift of a small **phoenix** emblem on a pendant. Apart from the phoenix representing new life arising from the fire of destruction (and I had just started listening to the Harry Potter book 'The Order Of The Phoenix' on tape!), in ancient Chinese culture it was the symbol of feminine (yin) energy; the symbol of masculine (yang) energy was the dragon. So within these few days the two complementary images came together as if to remind me of the January I Ching reading for the year ahead which spoke of the meeting of Heaven (male) and Earth (female).

S   **22nd October 2003: I received some junk mail from 'Luna' who promised me all kinds of joy ahead, if I sent her some money. It went into the bin of course. But on the way to the theatre that evening a new character named Luna was introduced in the Harry Potter book I was listening to. Then outside the theatre was the unusual registration number E 1 GHT, and on the way home I saw M 933 ARK which refers to the transfiguration.**

Suddenly I remembered that the lunar eclipse, which I had associated with the 'Dissolution' reading in January, was now imminent, as was the anniversary of my father's death. Three weeks after that there would be a solar eclipse too, on the eighth anniversary of moving into my new home. **I realised that I was now entering the Final Act of this drama**.

I made one more attempt with the I Ching to understand how things might develop with Bettina. I had asked the question only a week before so this was not a proper use of the book, but the circumstances were critical and the oracle clearly understood this, and let me off.

IC   **26th October 2003: Hexagram 55 is "Abundance", a time of outstanding greatness (which, one is warned, may not last long). The moving lines not only described our** relationship beautifully – "a union of clarity and energy" between two people "who suit each other" – but also its present difficulties – "one intent on greatness is overcome by darkness". The lines were completely consistent with the earlier readings: one must have great inner strength because "movement now is prohibited" and there will be a time of "total eclipse and darkness" when one cannot do anything (although is not to blame for the situation). Yet incredibly the outcome was Hexagram 40, "Deliverance" – the emergence from danger with difficulties and tensions resolved.

D   28th October 2003: two nights later the message was reinforced by another deeply emotional dream. I came out of a large country house and was showing someone the way around the side, but then I felt weak and collapsed. Several figures immediately came to help me; they were cheerful and supportive, I knew that they were 'spirits' and indeed I recognised one of my dead relatives. One of them carefully removed something from my mouth that was obstructing my breathing. A little later I recovered and left the gathering though I don't know where I went. I heard an uplifting song and returned to the others, running strongly up an escalator. The people were still there in the garden of the big house as if at a party, but they soon drifted away until I was left alone – with Bettina. Throughout the dream I kept seeing pages of typescript flashing in front of my eyes and also images of someone sewing something into the hem of a garment.

Leaving the house can symbolise a loss of safety – I was taking great risks in trying to 'find the way round' and it would prove too much for me. But even as I stumbled through this dark time, someone or something was reassuring me that I had spiritual support and that even beyond 'eclipse' there could be recovery (I also recalled the escalator dream of July 2002). I would be 'delivered'. I also gained a little strength this week by reading Paolo Coelho's book Manual Of The Warrior Of Light (that is, one who tries to follow a spiritual path).

All such 'warriors', he writes, make mistakes, experience fear and failure, lose the way and lose courage and sometimes believe in nothing... But the true warrior is open to God's guidance and never stops searching, he believes in miracles and ultimately is willing to face any danger.

I now wonder if the writing I saw in that last dream was a reference to what you are reading now, a draft of which was begun two months later. The sewing of a hem certainly suggested that things were close to being finished off... Yes, indeed.

S   **28ᵗʰ October 2003: On the way home I saw 798 DAN which is a reference to the final victory of the angels and to the majesty of God.**

But in the evening there was yet another Goodbye message from Bettina. So 'victory' in what sense then?

This was too much for me. When I arrived for work the next morning I collapsed with a serious panic attack; I had difficulty breathing, all the energy drained from me and I thought I was dying. Yesterday's dream had been a literal warning. Somehow I managed to telephone for help before giving way to it.

For the next two weeks I had little grasp on life, and slept for days. When awake, the light burned my eyes, I was only able to make shuffling movements and I was frightened of being among people. There were more attacks of breathing difficulty and of explosive migraine flashes, uncontrollable tearfulness and all the while a deep pain near my heart was draining my energy. My mind was flooded with wave upon wave of grief while simultaneously, and irrationally, it felt like a fire was raging through my inner consciousness. This, then, was the "Dissolution" and the "end of the day" foretold by the I Ching, the death I had been fearing. This was the eclipse.

I felt utterly alone as 'friends' melted away and the medical services proved (it seemed to me) pretty uncaring. Apart from Alice, who looked after me lovingly in the first few days (and, unknown to me, selflessly tried to persuade Bettina that she was the one I really needed), those near me who certainly did care just

169

couldn't cope with the intensity of it. In these moments I could see no future whatsoever. In any case, surely I had now done enough, tried hard enough? I'd changed my ways, tried to become more caring, brought up my son lovingly and fulfilled my job conscientiously.

Enough. I planned how I would die and rewrote my Will. The horoscope said that life **"may appear chaotic"** this week…

Φ

But something would just not let me go. Somewhere, love was still alive and my inner mind perversely insisted on believing in it. Only five days into this wilderness and one day before my father's anniversary, I had another strikingly optimistic dream!

D   **3rd November 2003: I was driving home on the A40 in London after a very long journey, a woman sitting happily beside me. We then turned right into a road I had lived in as a child in Wolverhampton, then right again into the drive of my old house. On the radio there was something funny about silly new laws being passed, such as it being illegal 'to be five feet away from a robin'. In high spirits, we started singing the old song 'Side By Side'.**

The dream was undoubtedly suggesting despite everything that I was approaching safety (home), that things were going 'right' and were improving (the road is called 'Highlands'). The song seemed to promise partnership while the robin is one of the most fortunate of all dream symbols, representing great happiness – in a period of 'five'? It was odd that the dream started in London on a road called The Westway, but this and the allusion to new laws seemed linked to my earlier dream in October about <u>West</u>minster Abbey which is of course across the road from the Houses of Parliament (though I still didn't understand it). The numbers involved, however, were extremely significant and referred to recent I Ching hexagrams: the house number is 49, "Revolution", and 40 is "Deliverance".

Where on earth was this *belief* coming from? It kept coming, too.

D   7th November 2003: I was back in a classroom after an absence from school, the atmosphere noisy but good-natured, and I felt strong and in control. The boys had just done a test and I had the answers prepared. A particular boy who'd been in trouble with me before showed me three books of his work – the third was very creative and colourful and I praised him for it. (I awoke from the dream with the song lyrics "You and me, always and forever..." running through my mind.)

Unfortunately, my conscious mind couldn't tell me what those 'answers' were! But it seemed that my 'test' was now over and that there *would* be an answer to it all – perhaps on the 'third' attempt (recalling the 'dating competition' dream). The waking song also suggested my belief, at least, in a secure and peaceful future.

The lunar eclipse was now upon us (the 8th November) and with it what some were calling a Harmonic Concordance – a Star of David alignment of planets. Astrologers described this as representing a time of intense expansion of spiritual awareness, of the unity of Heaven and Earth (as the I Ching had predicted for me) and a time for healing deeply felt emotional wounds... Important planetary patterns and events had accompanied several of my own significant moments in recent years and, very slowly, I began to see this terrible time in a different light. It seemed that my inner life was somehow coming into greater harmony with events in the outer world. Moreover, my breakdown could be seen as a life-changing *opportunity* – no, it was not something to be recommended, but it *was* a final clearing out of the old ways and a cleansing of the mind. What is this if not a healing of the old wounds? Some might call it an atonement. In its peculiar and unexpected way, it was exactly what I had set out to do eight years before and these events marked the ending of that path.

However, I have to say that it would be another <u>five</u> months before I would begin to feel that I was genuinely emerging from the wilderness. For the moment, I had very few answers, but perhaps someone else could help. The last time we met, Bettina had told me about "a loving and spiritual psychiatrist" whom she had met and she suggested that I see her. Her name was Davies (see my dream of 10th October!) and she was presently in Zambia, southern Africa (see my dream of 14th October!) and I made contact with her twenty days after that last dream. This seemed rather promising and I met her for the first time a week later.

S   11th November 2003: As I left this meeting, the car ... 20 JON was parked outside a nearby church. The text refers to "resurrection".

S   13th November 2003: I had just begun writing again, a draft of this account, and I wrote the passage describing the dream of 5th February that had predicted Bettina and ended with my 'knighthood'. I then went out for a walk to find, parked outside my house, the car with registration S 1 RNP.

This astonishing sign was a jolt, reminding me of the need for courage. In the next few days I suddenly did begin to feel more calm and strong, though still easily tired, as if drawing on some inner resources. Perhaps, too, I was receiving spiritual healing? As the solar eclipse and eighth anniversary approached, even the weekly horoscope became more optimistic again too, suggesting "**a big chance to make a fresh start in relationships...**"! That week I visited the Royal Observatory with a friend to deliver artwork and found that the place we had to go to was just a few feet from the **zero line of longitude**, marking 'a new beginning'. This reminded me that just the week before I had had a water meter installed at home; for the unconscious mind, the flow of water represents emotional life – I now had a fresh start, with my meter reset to **zero**! In the shop at Greenwich I also found a kaleidoscope (I hadn't seen one for years): the psychiatrist had used this just the week before as a symbol for breakdown, an opportunity to reform the pieces into which we have broken as a new, beautiful and more stable pattern.

It also seemed important to me now to visit the medium Grace again for a different sort of perspective on what was happening. Surely some spirit guidance was called for? I `phoned her but the only available appointment was at a time when I had a medical appointment already booked so I had to decline. Then ten minutes later my doctor's receptionist called to change the time of the medical! Someone or something was interfering and making things happen… *It proved to be a very significant meeting with Grace, but not for the reasons I had anticipated.* Once again she was extremely accurate in describing my circumstances and said that there was nothing I could do about the situation, it was just out of my hands (which was consistent with the I Ching). But I couldn't help feeling that much of what she said thereafter, though caring and well-meant, was of her own intuition rather than any spirit message; it was as if she couldn't make a proper 'connection'.

Even those horoscopes that had proved so revealing in recent months began to seem less and less relevant to me from now on. And when, with high hopes, I saw the psychiatrist again it only led to disappointment – shall I just say that she proved to be rather less 'loving and spiritual' than she had been billed… I found that I was going to have to get used to this sort of thing in the next few months. Perhaps the disturbances in my mind had caused some damage or had affected my psychic ability to connect with and receive information, help and guidance?

I began to realise that in almost every sense I really was on my own now.

Paolo Coelho has written of such defining moments in the spiritual life, of reaching a point where one must choose between **"leaving a familiar world wherein are stored all the things you ever wanted and for which you struggled long and hard"** and **"entering a dangerous, unfamiliar world where everything you have learned up until now will prove useless".** (Manual of the Warrior of Light, page 96.) One faces the truly daunting challenge of letting go of everything – and of everyone. If one is to continue to grow and to experience the depth of human life, to become more of what one can really be, then *one must risk it all.* It feels like nothing less than accepting the possibility of annihilation.

When one steps through that gateway to the new world, the new life, there are no paths to be seen, no lights or spirits or doctors to guide the way. There is, to begin with, only wilderness and shadow. This is the end of the day. Dissolution.

Φ

S   There is a curious footnote about finding one's new path. I have already described how the A41 road has held a particular significance in my life and dreams; I drive to work along a stretch of it every day. In the summer of 2003, the signs went up and the workmen arrived to embark upon "**major reconstruction works**" along the very section I use. I mused to myself that this seemed an entirely appropriate symbol for what I was anticipating – the climax of my path and renewal of my life… And it was encouraging that the signs promised "completion" before the end of the year.

The work was hugely inconvenient of course, this being a major trunk route into London, but as I sat in the morning queues I calmed myself with the thought that it was all spiritually inevitable and necessary! Everything would be seen to be worthwhile once the work was done.

But as time passed it became clear that all was not as it ought to be. Certainly, the road was duly resurfaced and the pavements renewed. The old central crash barriers were removed… but then nothing seemed to be taking their place and we commuters sat in our coned off crossover lanes wondering where all the workmen had gone. For long periods, absolutely nothing was being done. The road was dangerous now and there were daily jams and minor accidents. Moreover it was obvious that the work wasn't going to be finished anywhere near on time.

The events of my own life unfolded in parallel. Far from there being a smooth and happy transition to a new path, there was disruption, danger, frustration, delay and (apparently) broken promise. Throughout the winter, the A41 and I were strewn with rubble and incomplete sections!

By the New Year, the matter was just *so appropriately symbolic* that I got in touch with the contractors to find out what was happening. (Even that was suitably metaphorical since no-one in the various highway departments of various agencies seemed to know quite who was responsible and I was given several wrong names and telephone numbers.) It turned out that the original road signs had been misleading, or rather had not given the whole truth about the job; they only referred to the road surface and not to the replacement of the central barriers, or the reshaping of parts of the carriageway, which were "not due for completion until the end of May 2004"...

I therefore reasoned that my own new path would not be settled and 'safe' until the next summer. And after all, this was not the first time that signs had been incompletely understood.

X. *Winter*

In the approach to the terrible events of the autumn of 2003, my dreams, signs and readings were almost unfailingly encouraging. Yes, there were warnings of difficulties but <u>no</u> suggestion that I was heading in the wrong direction and should be prepared to change course (as I had experienced, for example, while with Dawn and Cathy). Indeed, I remain convinced that what happened was inevitable and necessary and *a natural part of the path*. My personal troubles with Bettina in no way undermine the fact that this relationship was the most important I had ever experienced and that with her I had touched the deepest levels of consciousness, of love, that I had ever known.

Of course there are times when we do 'go wrong' in situations and relationships, when we make significant mistakes; we must try to develop the self-awareness to recognise these and have the courage to do something about them. But just because we are hitting trouble doesn't of itself mean that we must have taken a wrong turn. These challenges can be the most important to us for our spiritual growth. Recognising what *kind* of trouble we're in, however, can be incredibly difficult: it's what being an aware and caring human being is all about. So the signposts are there to help!

Along with the warnings, I had also received a good deal of reassurance that I would be 'safe' (see especially the huge dream of 3rd October). And now, before the winter set in, a few further powerful clues presented themselves as if to strengthen me for the journey into the unknown ahead.

S   **21st November 2003: Just two days before the solar eclipse and the eighth anniversary of my new home, I received an offer out of the blue to do some badly needed roof repairs to my house at low cost. I had been worried about this and simply could not have afforded the job in the normal way. This event represented 'renewed security'.**

S   **23rd November 2003: The weekly horoscope (this was the last one that seemed at all appropriate for a considerable** time) promised that "one issue really gets... sorted out. Somehow the truth will come out... associated with your attitudes towards a partner..."

Alice knew how significant this anniversary was for me and came round to keep me company. But for all that we had shared in recent years and despite her caring for me while I was ill, it was now quite evident that we were on entirely different paths. After our goodbye, that same night brought another detailed, beautiful and optimistic dream.

D   24th November 2003: I was on a long journey with a woman, first by bus and then by riverbus. It seemed that we might miss our connection to a ship for our ocean voyage ahead, so we got off and went on by foot. The woman was heavily pregnant and I was loaded down with our luggage. At dusk we came to a river, its banks flooded and muddy, which we had to cross. I called out and a man on the other side came to fetch us in a rowing boat; he was silent but friendly. On the way across we passed through a kind of marketplace where we saw baby clothes for sale and I talked about buying some for us. Then the water became shallow so to make things easier I got out of the boat, dragging our heavy box through a small square doorway before reaching the other side of the water. There I waited for the woman to join me, knowing that all was well and that we would make our connection safely. I heard the happy voices of people enjoying themselves and a small light came on nearby, shining into my eyes.

This is a classic 'spiritual journey' dream describing the stages through which we have to pass, the anxieties and the struggles with our load, but also suggesting that there is help from 'the other side'. Moreover, despite the time of separation, there is a promise of 'rebirth' and deliverance, and a solution (the light) to our problems. Possibly, I thought, the symbol of pregnancy might be a clue as to when I might reach the other side of my present difficulties – nine months hence?! But I also knew that what I must accept is that the dream did not necessarily promise the rebirth of one *particular*

178

relationship; rather, it was reassuring me of the development of a more secure and peaceful emotional life. That may or may not be focused on a special person. Each of us has our own individual path and our own choices to make along the way, and we can never force others to follow our chosen route.

Surely it is the frustration of our own personal desires and our attachments that cause our suffering – so we must learn to let go of them and surrender to the guidance we receive.

This is not to say that we should give up on our ambitions, or not fight with all our strength for what we dearly believe in. But our thoughts and feelings and words and actions must always be mindful, with the honest intention of caring for others. Living with the heart means to love life and ourselves and others, and it cannot be loving if we impose our will and desires on them.

So however much it may have been my instinct to interpret the dream in terms of a future with Bettina, I recognised that this powerful experience in these given circumstances was the point at which I must finally give way to God's will. Of course I will not manage it, being as flawed as any other human being by personal weakness and ignorance and a hugely egoistic belief in my own identity and self-importance. Like any other recalcitrant child at school, I shall no doubt have to learn the lesson over and over again. But for the moment, at least, the teaching did seep in and I became more peaceful.

And this is the point of my book! When we do let go, there is spiritual guidance and renewed strength.

S   25th November 2003: The next day, 'by coincidence', I heard a BBC radio programme about the storms that beset our lives.

Mystics and spiritual teachers throughout history agree, it was said, that when the tempest rages we must not fight it but try just to be still. The storm has purpose. Perhaps it comes to change our direction or to clear the air and purge us of our falsehoods. It humbles us. The story of Elijah, I think, is among the most inspiring of all: rejected, betrayed, in pain and despair, he received the most wonderful angelic guidance. Yet he was still a man for all that and continued to be wracked by doubt. Ultimately, it was in the calm *after* the storm that 'God came to him' and brought him to triumph.

Φ

"WHEN THE STORM BREAKS" (a song)

When the storm breaks, waves like mountains, darkness closing in...
Hard to breathe much less believe a new life can begin.

Trying to find your way home on a winding path, running away out of sight,
Searching the shadows for footholds, keeping your eyes on a small distant light,
And just when you think you're secure, you find yourself outside a door
That you've never seen before.

You turn to run but the storm has begun and you can't find a way to return,
Yet how can you leave everything you believed in and let go of all that you learned?
You've lost everything that you owned and stand there entirely alone,
Facing the unknown.

Now is the time to hold on, now is the time not to fall,
It's the hardest thing you've ever done, doing nothing at all...
Reach for the spirit within, lose your desire to win,
And a new life will begin.

When the storm breaks, waves like mountains, darkness closing in...
Hard to breathe much less believe a new life will begin.

Φ

S　26th November 2003: I started back at work today. On my way home I saw ... 121 DAN. Chapter 12, verse 1 of the Book of Daniel promises that at "...a time of great suffering... you will be delivered."

In the first few days of December, two extremely strange things happened.

D　1st December 2003: There was a long and confusing dream, but all I could remember later was that it involved my sister and that when she left I was with Bettina. However, I awoke with the absolutely insistent thought that "Pleiades" was very important.

I had to look it up. This is the name of a cluster of stars in Taurus, also known as "the Seven Sisters"; I also learned the curious fact that only six of the stars are visible, one being hidden behind others. It seemed that the dream and waking experience were suggesting some kind of cryptic clue about my family life, though I didn't understand it. However, just one week later:

S　8th December 2003: I received on my computer a fragment of an email sent to Alice by her son during a trip abroad. Checking with her later, I found that the message had been sent to her several months earlier though I have no idea how an incomplete section of it arrived on my screen now (I'm told it may be due to some kind of virus). The telling point is that the fragment, just two sentences, described "six people in the group plus the guide".

This had an uncanny resonance with the Pleiades experience and was virtually a repetition of the 'clue'. It may have been a genuinely random event; but its undoubted synchronicity with the dream suddenly made a new connection in my mind. Both events described a group of six people plus one other, while the links to Alice and my sister suggested that they were women. Now I also remembered the dreams of April 2002 in which 'two fours' (representing the two important periods of my path) had merged to form a pattern with six significant points, this number being repeated for emphasis. I realised that *there had been six important emotional relationships with women in my life* (not counting my mother, who nonetheless of course influenced them all psychologically). Bettina was the sixth, at the climax of my spiritual journey, and the deepest experience of them all. It seemed that these events were reassuring me of our place in each other's destiny.

During this week there was one other dream, but it was of the sort that has to be felt to be understood.

D   4ᵗʰ December 2003: I had been away somewhere, attending some kind of 'spiritual convention'. During a free afternoon, I walked down a certain road I know and looked around a shop of magical artefacts and antiques, seeking something particular but unable to find what I wanted. (There is no such shop on that road.) Then I returned to where I was staying where I observed myself sleeping. There followed some scenes in which I gave and received healing, and then I met my father who was caring towards me and promised that I would be safe.

This was not so much a dream as a journey on some deep inner mental plane, and I awoke feeling as if I'd travelled far, far away and met with beings in a different world. As I came to, my whole body and brain were flashing with electrical energy as if having difficulty readjusting to being physical, though my thoughts were calm and clear. I could also very definitely still feel other 'beings' nearby, as realistically as one does in the normal world. The experience was deeply moving. I shall never know the truth of it, but its meaning was clear enough: there were no 'magical solutions' to my present situation, there just had to be a time of rest and recovery.

And so it proved. Almost from this very point I seemed to lose the ability to access those other states of consciousness wherein I had been receiving so much paranormal information on an almost daily basis. Life became much more ordinary and less intense. This was actually rather hard to deal with, since I felt that I was now setting out quite alone on an entirely new journey with very few signposts. Apart from one psychological 'therapy dream' in early

January – **a car journey in which I found myself in the wrong lane but managed to turn back the right way, only to find myself on an unfamiliar road before again being able to move back onto the correct one, finally arriving at my destination, a stadium where I was given a refund and change** – I remembered virtually no more dreams for more than three months. I still noted small synchronicities and registrations and they helped to keep my spirits up but, frankly, they usually weren't very informative. This was new territory indeed!

But the turn of the year still held a couple of astonishing surprises for me before, as it were, the winter set in.

S   **23rd December 2003: Just before Christmas I took a gift to Bettina's house and left it outside. Yes, despite everything I wanted to express my love. Hoping that she might respond once she saw it, instead of going home I decided to find a local pub and wait for an hour. I didn't know the area well so went into the first place I found along the road, a fairly rough and noisy 'local'. It was quite a big place but I could only find one free table at the far end of the lounge. Sitting there on the table, as incongruous in this place as it could be, was a knight chess piece. There was no sign of any other pieces anywhere else in the place. Recalling my dream of the previous February that had predicted meeting Bettina, this brought tears to my eyes. And then the nearby television began playing the song The Power of Love.**

No, she did not respond. But that little piece of wood spoke volumes about the need for courage and determination on this path.

IC   **1st January 2004: My habitual question for the year ahead yielded Hexagram 2, "The Receptive". This is the archetypal description of the feminine (yin) qualities of devotion, gentleness and calm perseverance. In this state one does not take strong action or seek to make things happen, but is instead quietly receptive to guidance. The moving line described the onset of darkness and of cold, as in winter, the time of "dissolution"** – my present state. (That is, there is nothing that can be done but wait. This was echoed in a reading concerning Bettina the next day which described our inability to move forward and the need for inner resolve.) But to what does this lead? There is a natural cycle to our lives and there will always be change, just as winter must give way to spring when "the darkness is past and the light returns" and there is "a natural transformation of the old ways to the new". The resulting hexagram was number 24, "Return − the Turning Point".

You may perhaps be wondering about my Christmas cracker 'sign' this year… Especially after the last one, I approached the dining table with some trepidation this time and even considered ignoring the cracker − well, I didn't know how much more I could take just now. In the event, it contained **a plastic alphabet stencil**, which I immediately associated with writing.

You're reading it!

Φ

Throughout this account I have been using the metaphor of life being a 'journey' and the unfolding of a 'path'. Some of you may think that this is not entirely reasonable, and may put unnecessary restraints on the way we think about our experiences. So I'd like here to explore this idea further, so that we may perhaps understand better some of the things that happen when we try to live more consciously.

A 'journey' implies a definite destination, whereas none of us really knows what that might actually be at all. Moreover, while there may be many alternative routes to a destination, the metaphor implies that some of these must be good and worthwhile while others are clearly bad or in the wrong direction. But at the end of the day, as it were, it may not matter all that much which way we went or how long it took us or how many mistakes we made in getting there, as long as we arrive. Perhaps we could say, then, that life is an *exploration* rather than a journey.

In metaphysical terms, many spiritual thinkers have described the process of human life as 'a return to the Source' or as achieving 'oneness with God' or 'cosmic consciousness' for example. It seems inevitable that we should assume some sort of end-state, for as rational beings we are driven by goals and by problem-solving as a means of achieving them. If we want to achieve something through our careers (whether it be status, power, financial security, personal satisfaction etc) then we adopt strategies that will lead towards those aims such as gaining qualifications or experience or personal contacts. If our goal is to achieve a contented family life then we must try to understand and care for those who are close to us, balance our needs with theirs, provide a secure environment, perhaps establish a support network of friends and relatives, and so on. These processes are often unconscious, but nonetheless we all have such goals and we are the more successful in achieving them – which is to say *happier* – the more mindful we are of our own nature and in our relationships with others. If we are mindless, we tend to hurt and alienate others and we achieve little happiness.

I suggest that much the same applies to our spiritual goals, however we might phrase them. Although there are those who would argue that spirituality has little to do with reason (supposing it to be somehow a 'higher' way of being), surely we cannot deny our nature as rational beings who live in a material world. There can be no virtue in trying to ignore or to transcend these facts of life. Not only would this be an abnegation of our basic responsibility of care, towards ourselves and the others who share our world, it would be the ultimate insult to God.

Alternatively, of course, you could deny the existence of *any* God or of *any* spiritual purpose in life, but then you're probably not reading this book. Purposelessness is not far removed from mindlessness, with similar consequences.

So if we do adopt a sense of spiritual purpose, then we are setting goals and we must be at least as thoughtful and careful in our strategies towards achieving these as we would be in, say, our careers – actually more so, for the destination is much less obvious. Moreover, there is a great deal more that we *don't know* about our minds than, say, we do know about business practice.

A spiritual approach to life *is* then, surely, an exploration and a kind of journey, and we should go about it in that manner.

Nigel Peace

Suppose I am going on a driving holiday from my home in London to the south of France. This analogy will of course be flawed but it might be fun to look out for the useful bits of it. Now, I know where I'm starting from and I have a fairly definite goal - I might even have booked it. I also have a limited time in which to achieve it since I have other responsibilities back home (family, a career, a cat...). *If the trip is to be enjoyable* then there are certain things I need to do before I even set out, such as service the car, look at some maps, book a ferry and perhaps buy insurance, pack some clothes and food and ensure I have money available. If I don't do some of this preparation then there is certainly a risk of serious frustration on the trip that might make it unhappy or even worthless.

When at last I set out, I could of course head north towards Birmingham. When and if I do arrive in France, I could of course head east towards Belgium. Such excursions are certainly possible and could even be quite interesting in their own way, but they are not helpful in getting me where I want to go; they might even ultimately prevent me from getting there at all since I would lose time, run the risk of mishaps or getting lost, and I might miss my ferry. Suppose instead that I have got myself into France and am driving south (with some caution since the road layout and customs are unfamiliar), there is still a variety of routes that I could take. Motorways are fast and easy but a bit expensive and not very interesting. Trunk roads show me more of the country and its towns and people but are slower and will involve more stopovers and costs. Either way I am going to have to read maps and understand signs; even so there is a chance that I will miss or not understand the signs (or there may not be any when I need them) and I could get lost. In this case, some knowledge of the language is going to be useful, so that I can ask for help. Getting to my destination enjoyably and safely, then, involves a good deal of preparation, thoughtfulness, care and learning along the way. There could be some great unplanned adventures too: it might be a good thing not to have my mind so fixed on the south of France that I miss out on some of the other pleasures that the rest of France has to offer en route.

Probably the most obvious flaw in this analogy is that, spiritually, most of the time we don't know where we're going!

There are those, of course, who believe that they do know exactly what our destination is, and some even claim to have booked a place there by virtue of their membership of a particular faith – they've bought some insurance. My only observation to this is that if such arrogant certainty were possible then life would be entirely unnecessary.

It is the essence of being human that we do not entirely know what it means to be human.

But on the other hand, neither are we totally vague about our destination. We have the testimony of those who have gone before us and who can offer us, if not maps as such, at least images of how the journey may unfold. We can prepare ourselves in the setting out, and check ourselves along the way, by referring to this literature and teaching; our learning must be critical though, for there are many misleading guidebooks written by rather too self-interested authors. Fortunately we also have our own instincts to guide us – we are all spiritual beings, after all, with some degree of inner awareness. And provided that we take care of ourselves, so as to be healthy in body, mind and heart (we service our vehicle), then we can trust that awareness to help us along the way. Taking care of ourselves is important. We must develop our personal resources (the equivalent of spare clothes, food and money), for this trip into the largely unknown could well require mental strength and flexibility, calmness under pressure and perhaps courage. We shouldn't set out until we know we are ready.

But although we may often be unsure about the road and where it leads, and even about our own ability to continue following it, surely the most important attribute for us to pack is our *attitude* to the journey, one of purposefulness and caring about *being the best that we can possibly be*. We must *want* to be good and loving people and to develop our minds fully, to be open to others and what they have to teach us, to treat others as we would wish to be treated. If we are seeking an ultimate goal of happiness and peacefulness, we have no hope of achieving it unless these principles guide our every step and we try to develop them in all our thoughts and feelings and words and actions. Gosh, how difficult is that?! This expedition is certainly a challenge.

Suppose that we are now 'on the way'. Is there an equivalent of having 'a limited time' available to us? Well, we just don't know! Certainly, many of the precognitive experiences that I have described suggest that we have a very incomplete notion of the nature of time anyway. My synchronistic experiences (not to mention the enormous body of evidence now in support of, for example, telepathy and clairvoyance) further suggest that human consciousness extends far beyond the normally accepted limits of materialism. Some will undoubtedly take this as evidence for the existence of a human soul that endures beyond physical death. I can only repeat that *we just cannot know this.*

So rather than adopting the comforting attitude that it really doesn't matter what we do or how much we mess up because there'll always be another chance for us later, in Heaven or by reincarnation, it is surely more responsible to assume that we may only have this one lifetime. So we should do everything we can to make the most of it and of ourselves. Whether it is true or not, the mindful way *is* to think of ourselves as material beings with limited time. We also have limited resources and abilities. And of course we also have down to earth responsibilities to others that limit our personal freedom. The implications of this are that we cannot just wander about aimlessly on our journey, as it were via Birmingham or Belgium, and there certainly are wrong directions to beware of. Hopefully we can recognise these by our loss of sense of purpose, or by noticing that we or others are being hurt avoidably and without good reason.

But clearly there are many possible alternative right directions. No-one has the authority to say that one particular path is the true or correct one. It is for each individual to find his or her own way according to one's interests and abilities and *needs.* The alternative roads of France all offer their own joys and discoveries, though if we do know something about what we want or need to experience this will guide us to some of the appropriate places. Again, we can prepare ourselves by heeding the advice of others who have gone before, especially if they warn us of particular hazards that we are likely to meet – the storms, the roadworks, the Channel…!

Our trip is now proceeding apace but we are in foreign territory where a great deal is unfamiliar to us. **This is where the signs become so important**. Sometimes they give us really important information such as which particular turning to take onto a new road, or about some danger lying just ahead - we may have to slow down or give way or stop for a while. Sometimes they tell us how far it is to the next recognisable landmark. Sometimes they are almost incidental and merely tell us that we are on the right road, which is nonetheless reassuring. The synchronicities and omens that I have described fall into each of these categories. *Such signs, however small, are available to all of us and are immensely helpful.*

However, while many of them are simple and clear and abundant (although your particular trip might be through, say, the Sudan rather than France), many of them will be in a foreign language and involve words or idioms that are totally unfamiliar. Obviously, this is not a reason to ignore them! How small-minded is the materialist who rejects the paranormal or mystical because it doesn't fit comfortably into his present knowledge. The first purpose in writing this book is to show that there are many different signs to guide us and that *we can learn to understand them.* On our journey through France we would gradually come to know the meanings of what we observe and become familiar with the way things are done there. How much more important, then, is it that we should be prepared to look for and learn the meanings of the symbolism and signs that our minds present to us on the most important journey we can ever undertake, the discovery of the soul?

However, despite all this rational stuff about purposefulness and preparation and experiential learning, let's admit that it is virtually inevitable that *at some point we will get lost.* Reason alone will simply not be enough, for the exploration we are on is through lands far stranger than France.

Even France can be bad enough. At the very outset of my own odyssey described here, I actually did take a holiday trip to France; and although I was in fact fairly familiar with the country and its language, this time I planned a new route that would take me close to Paris in the early hours of the morning. But despite my maps and notes and normally good sense of direction I was, like so many others, defeated by the Peripherique! It was an extraordinary and unsettling experience: there came a point where I simply had to stop the car in a layby and admit that I had absolutely no idea where I was or which direction to go. It was dark and there was no-one about. Fortunately I had packed a sandwich and a flask, which were comforting, and I silently prayed for some kind of help. After a short while another car pulled in just ahead of me, the French driver apparently taking a rest, so I approached him with my map and haltingly asked for directions. He didn't tell me which way to go. Instead, he smiled and said "Follow me", then led me for twenty minutes back to the junction I needed before turning round with a wave and disappearing.

Was that man not an angel? This was one of the most important lessons I have ever learned and it came precisely at the time I needed it. We do get confused and lost, and however brilliant our minds there are limits to what we can know by reasoning. But if we can remain calm and humble and open, then guidance comes to lead us back to our path. This may be from some spiritual source beyond our understanding, but it may equally be from an ordinary stranger in the street. So should we not all be prepared to offer whatever support we can to others on their journeys?

Φ

The reason for the philosophical excursion of the last few pages is to put in context the final part of this account, the early months of 2004. I had embarked upon a deliberate spiritual journey with particular purposes and experienced many wonderful and some terrible things, joyful and painful, and I had received much phenomenal guidance along the way. But one of the strangest aspects of it all, perhaps, was the gradual realisation that there was a definite pattern and period to it. It was an intensive journey of eight years with an identifiable rhythm: two equal halves, four learning relationships of certain lengths and with repeating challenges, and so on. I would not suggest that every spiritual path can be described in this way; but it may be fair to observe that there can be definite periods in our lives when we need or have the opportunity to learn particular things, so we should try to be alert to what the events of our lives are challenging us with. [5]

I would also not suggest that I had successfully learned everything I needed to know on my path, or that my work was done! Actually I feel that I failed in several important respects and that I shall have to repeat certain classes. Having read this far, I'm sure you will agree! But there are limits to what we can achieve and to what we can endure. Life is a continuous cycle of change and *nothing* stays the same forever. Whatever my personal desires for my life, that period needed to end, facing me with a new path and new challenges.

As Paolo Coelho says, I had to pass through that doorway and enter "a dangerous and unfamiliar world..." - just at the time when I wanted a good rest! Having done my best in France, as it were, I was perhaps crossing into Italy where I've never driven before and know hardly any of the language.

At and near the frontier there were still some recognisable signs to encourage me, which I described earlier in this chapter. So I felt that I was safely heading in the right direction and, even if I didn't quite know where I was going, I wasn't exactly lost. The fact remains, however, that I was in very new territory and in keeping with that I was simply *unable to remember any significant dreams* for virtually three months; moreover, life became very ordinary and uneventful. Sometimes this was worrying – had I lost contact with the inner consciousness? Not at all. Learning from the patterns of our experience, we have to recognise that there will always be periods of rest or consolidation or perhaps even retreat when we can do little but wait quietly and with inner resolve, having little apparent influence in the world. The seasons come when they will and we cannot make them do otherwise, however frustrated we feel and

---

[5] Of course, like the school student who is not yet comfortable with quadratic equations, we can choose not to accept the challenge even if we do recognise it, for we may not be ready for it yet. It does require a certain confidence and preparation. Moreover, our circumstances may not allow it if, for example, we have important responsibilities towards others. It is still a good thing to recognise that there *are* lessons for our souls that we shall need to meet sooner or later.

however we try to force them. In February 2004 I even attempted to 'move things on' deliberately by doing the same sort of clearing and cleaning work that had seemed so symbolic and successful the previous year – to absolutely no avail!

On the other hand, at such times there are still *some* signposts along the path to let us know that we are heading the right way. They may be sparse and often not very informative, but they are there. Here are a few examples:

S   **5th January 2004: I started an evening course in Raja Yoga meditation, hoping that this would help me to keep a peaceful mind during these difficult days, and on the way to the first session I saw the registration …RAJ. During the next week or so I saw different …RAJ or R…AJA plates three times, …REX twice (both raja and rex mean 'king') and …TAO twice.** After the course ended I did not seen a single …RAJ again for months. These signs are of the 'not very helpful yet reassuring' type.

S   **11th February 2004: My computer again received that same stray piece of email message described on 8th December 2003. On the same day I started listening on the radio to a serialised book about precognition, called The Probable Future.** These synchronicities seem more like 'deliberate messages of support'.

S   **13th March 2004: Just as I was writing the section of this account which dealt with my breakdown, my computer crashed! It turned out to be a rare but serious fault which took quite a while to get fixed and which delayed my writing considerably. This may have been just a weird coincidence, but with hindsight later I saw that it was not such a bad thing – I needed a little more perspective on the last few months before describing them.** Perhaps this kind of synchronicity illustrates that our minds are somehow very much connected with our physical environment.

D   17th **March 2004: At last, another dream! I observed myself overlooking a large area of ground that had just been completely cleared in preparation for rebuilding.** My unconscious mind seemed to be encouraging me that my life was now ready to start moving forward again.

S   17th **March 2004: This same day I saw the registrations ...RWP (my father's initials), then ...NEW and ...LYF together; later I saw S...HOK and ...ANS.** The first group of these was in harmony with my dream while the others suggested some surprising news ahead (in maths we write 'Ans' as short for Answer).

S   18th **March 2004: The next day I saw M 869 ARK which refers to one of Christ's miracles. That evening I indeed received some wonderful and extremely unexpected family news – my daughter had decided to be baptised.** The signs of these two days were therefore actually precognitive.

S   1st **April 2004: I saw the number plate JOY... and just a few minutes afterwards received a completely unexpected and nice text message from Bettina. Later the same day I finally received my computer back, now mended – the breakdown was over!** Both a precognition and a neat synchronicity to encourage me that somehow all would be well.

S   3rd **April 2004: I arrived home to find the car ...CLU parked outside my house. Once indoors I settled down to work through a previously unseen A Level revision exercise, preparing answers for my students. Question six was about the Pleiades stars!** I had taken the original dream about this on 1st December 2003 to be some kind of 'clue' about Bettina's importance in my life. Was this synchronicity perhaps reassuring me of that?

During these few months there were many other such instances, most of them just generally reassuring although a few more were definite advance warnings, about mistakes I might make in daily life or, notably in the last week of April, about some nastiness coming my way from others. One may perhaps question whether there is any purpose in receiving such notice if the unpleasant situation cannot be prevented. Well, for one thing it does help to prepare one's mind, to be calm and resolved, especially when one has learned to trust such signs as I have.

But the real significance of it is that this sort of event simply shouldn't happen at all according to conventional wisdom. The now demonstrable fact that precognition of any sort is not only possible but can occur regularly completely shatters our common understanding of the nature of time and of the relationship between mind and body.

Naturally I was giving a great deal of thought to these ideas now as well as reading about others' research and theories. This effort was eventually rewarded by one final (for now) dream that seems, to me, utterly conclusive.

D   **18ᵗʰ April 2004: I dreamed that I was a man who had dreamed something very important, then woken up and recorded it. But during the telling of the dream to others he was interrupted by someone challenging it. He then went back to sleep and had another dream which confirmed the first. He woke up knowing that this was of great significance for many people.**
I actually woke up at this point and thought about the dream in a hazy, semiconscious way. But then I drifted back to sleep and experienced *the exact same dream again*, identical in every way except that this time the main character was a woman.

Most interpreters agree that to dream of dreaming is to access a very deep level of consciousness wherein lies our most esoteric and fundamental understanding of life – a spiritual awareness beyond the psychological. Moreover, for a dream to be repeated exactly is a clear indication of its absolute importance; this is information that *has* to get through.

Consider the content: there is a dream, an awakening and a challenge, then another dream that confirms the first. Then I *did* wake up and challenge (analyse) it before the entire dream was

194

repeated, and this repetition was a confirmation of the first dream. **So the first dream was a clear precognition of my waking and then having the second dream.**

There is another momentous element to this experience. It is commonly argued by sceptics, and not without some justification, that to remember and record a dream (which later turns out to seem to be precognitive) is to set in motion thought processes that eventually bring about the events described in the dream. In other words, the dream is not a genuine precognition; instead, *having the dream causes the events.* I think this may well have some truth to it in the case of what I have earlier called 'wishful' or 'therapy' dreams: on the inner levels of our minds we may be programming ourselves to think and behave in future in certain ways that will bring about what we want or need. It is the same sort of thing that we might do in our conscious lives through, say, 'positive thinking' or 'affirmations'. This seems very healthy, provided that we don't try to force others to think or behave according to our own desires.

But on the other hand I think I have shown with many of the accounts in this book that dreams can often foretell events (i) of which no-one has any knowledge or control over at the time, and (ii) which were entirely beyond my own influence anyway. The last pair of dreams described is a succinct illustration of this. **My having the first dream cannot have 'caused' the second because the first dream contained an account of the second – it had already happened.**

Is this not a logical proof of precognition, of something that should be entirely impossible if time is linear (proceeding from the known past to the unknown future at a steady rate)?

Φ

I want to suggest to you that the experiences described in this book (all of which, with very many others, are fully documented) clearly demonstrate two things:

1. **Human beings are able to access knowledge and guidance that help to promote our psychological and spiritual growth, by means beyond our normal senses (in my case through dreams, synchronicities and the I Ching). This may also imply that the individual human mind is connected, at some alter state of consciousness, with other minds.**

2. **Our common notion of time is wrong. It *is* certainly helpful in our physical lives to think of time as linear, and we make sense of events by their being in succession; the idea that an 'effect' follows a 'cause' is fundamental to our success as a species. This notion is not false but it is *limited*, in the same way that to think of ourselves as purely physical is limited. We own states of consciousness that are entirely non-physical and in those the 'future' exists 'now'.**

   To the extent that a future event can be perceived now, some have even argued that the future is therefore a cause of our present awareness, the effect. This is of course non-sense because it breaks the rules of our definitions of the words used. We simply don't, yet, have words adequately to describe the true nature of time. Similarly, precognition does *not* mean that our experience is wholly predetermined either, because the very word 'predetermined' presupposes linear time!

   Aren't human beings the most *wonderful* things?

XI. *Deliverance*

Above all else I have wanted this account to focus on the nature of the spiritual guidance that I have received – the dreams, the synchronicities and so on – and the ways in which they have helped me to change and to grow. This is because I believe that *everyone* can access this kind of guidance and thus better find the way on their own path.

But of course a very personal story, a love story, has also been described because it has been through the challenges and joys of close emotional relationships that I have mostly been learning what I needed to learn. So although this book is not meant to be about 'me', it seems reasonable to 'complete' the story... I am conscious that the two aspects of the account are obviously closely connected.

Some may object that: "Well, his love life didn't work out very well did it, despite all the belief, so how can anyone trust this so-called guidance?"

What does it mean for a relationship to 'work out' – do they all have to live happily ever after? That might be nice. And I suppose in our hearts we all hope for that kind of peace and contentment, though surely we know how unrealistic it is in this world of change and contrast, this life full of challenges where we are bombarded by information, outside influences and high expectations. And in any case, each of us has a different path and different lessons. Some are blessed with emotional security. Many are not.

Yes, at the end of 2003 I felt a deep loneliness and sadness because it seemed that I had lost Bettina, the woman I loved more deeply and with whom I had touched a more profound joy than anything I had known before. I had never felt so close to another person. I had never believed myself capable of such experience. She was, perhaps, the proof of the transformation I had sought. And so I began to realise that rather than feel sad I should instead give thanks for our time together. If this was all we were to have, then it was still very, very beautiful.

But it wasn't all. And there was more to learn!

197

Nigel Peace

Φ

You may remember that at the very time that things were breaking up so painfully, indeed even at the darkest hours, I was still experiencing dreams and other guidance that reassured me of a happy resolution, of healing and of 'victory'. This seemed quite perverse – surely it was just wishfulness? And yet despite the horror I found that I felt no anger whatsoever and no sense of recrimination, just the same simple love. I was in pain, but my belief was unshaken (though it was now to face the greatest challenge of all).

For almost a year there was virtually no contact between the two of us and very few signs of encouragement: as I described in the last chapter, the psychic and spiritual activity I had become so accustomed to just calmed down to a mere shadow of what it had been. For example, in ten months I only remembered twenty-two dreams of any kind. I know that my experience was on a much lesser scale, but I imagined that I could identify in a way with hostages in a war zone – suffering apparently innocently, the future entirely uncertain, receiving no news or reason to hope, holding on to whatever one believes in…

There *were* still car registrations and synchronicities to observe, but I came to realise that they were more reflections in the outer world of my inner state of mind, of my continuing belief, rather than messages or predictions. Just as dreams can be of different types and qualities (described in Chapter I), I began to see more clearly that the same is true of 'signs'; indeed, **perhaps signs are simply a form of waking dream**. They are not all to be taken at face value, but with pinches of salt, and great discrimination is needed when deciding how meaningful they are. So for a whole six months there was little that took this story forward.

I concentrated on my career and my home and gradually regained my strength. In the spring I decided that I needed more social contact so I joined a dating agency, hoping for some friendship – there wouldn't be any romantic relationship since my heart wasn't in it. On the other hand, being a mere man, there were moments when I couldn't help wondering… Then on one such day,

I was shaken by a powerful dream reminding me of what was important.

D   19th May 2004: I was at a railway station, trying to buy vegetables from a woman. She gave me far too little change, but when I confronted her she seemed not to understand me and unable to communicate. I decided to take her to the station manager to sort it out, but found that I had to take a guide dog with me too!

So I am on my journey but for the moment 'stationary', unable to move forward. I am seeking some kind of emotional 'nourishment' (from other women), trying to make 'changes' but getting it wrong – these attempts are ill-conceived and I shall not achieve any real communication thus. *I must allow myself to be guided by a higher spiritual authority.*

Within days this apparent 'message' was backed up by further reassurance of the true path.

S   26th May 2004: I had left a small gift at Bettina's house to mark Shavuot and immediately afterwards saw the car M 289 ARK, a reference to the healing of a paralysed man. This was closely followed by the car BET …!

S   27th May 2004: on the way to a public function I saw two different cars with registration … TRU. Across a crowded hall at the function I saw Bettina, and my heart reminded me of the truth.

S   31st May 2004: driving near her home I saw the (personalised) number plate … 5OUL followed immediately by M 261 ARK which refers to forgiveness.

D   31st May 2004:
(1) I saw several women's faces and associated with them somehow was the number 44. Then the numbers changed to 43.

(2) I drove to a country restaurant, for the second time, for an important date but had difficulty parking in the small triangular area available. There was a space but it was unavailable because of roadworks, while another space was too dangerous to enter due to a step in the road surface. But I managed to move some tables and parked. Inside I saw a friend named Moore. Then I met a beautiful woman with whom I was very close, but our meeting was rushed and incomplete. Later I met her again in the same place and this time the feeling between us was good and powerful. At one point she turned completely upside down! Then I was with a young man watching a television screen, which was also a computer; the young man switched from watching a film about time travel to using the computer for planning a sports and exercise programme that he was going to study.

The night before these dreams I had prayed for guidance concerning Bettina: she was filling my heart but was not in my life – how was this to change? The first dream seemed to refer me back to the previous path of 4 + 4 years and relationships that had reached a zenith with her. The result of all of this was 43, the I Ching hexagram of 'Breakthrough' that I had received almost a year earlier. This dream reaffirmed to me that I was heading in the right direction, *that all was as it should be.*

The second dream gave a more detailed description of things and a prediction. Our first relationship had been a difficult and unsettled time (seeking 'nourishment', the parking problem, an 'incomplete meeting') and there was 'work to be done'; but there would be a second chance, 'more' to come, in fact a complete 'turn around' in the situation. 'Time travel' and 'tele-vision' both suggest looking ahead to the future. I felt that the young man here was my son who indeed would be going to study sports science at university in four months time. Is that when things would change, in the autumn?

In June, nearly eight months after my illness, I felt at last that a corner had been turned and I had recovered my strength and composure. My birthday I Ching reading was simply **Hexagram 45: "Gathering Together"** – the work has been done, now is a

great time of unification and achievement. More colloquially, things would now start to 'come together'. I knew that I just had to be *patient*, though for all my experiences this has always been so difficult for me! Yet every so often there would appear another set of extraordinary synchronicities to uplift me…

S   **29th June 2004: my weekly internet horoscope gave the very unusual prediction that "You might feel that…your guardian angels are delivering special messages to you. You could experience some exciting coincidences…" That morning I also saw the car number … BET.**

S   **30th June 2004: next day I was listening in my car to a recording of 'Earthly Powers' by Anthony Burgess. A priest was speaking about "great coincidence" and his sixth sense, and then I saw again the same … BET. This was in an entirely different location to yesterday's sighting, and I had never seen this car before.**

S   **2nd July 2004: now came one of the most incredible synchronicities I have ever experienced. I was printing off a copy of this manuscript when a good friend called in for a chat; we were talking about my feelings for Bettina when the computer printer suddenly jammed at the very page that describes the beautiful beginning of the relationship! (This printer has never jammed before or since.)**

At such moments it is really difficult not to believe in some sort of divine and deliberate spiritual intervention. There was a feeling that for a timeless split second the universe had stopped and I was in a peaceful place of pure understanding. Whether this is an altered state of consciousness or indeed contact with a higher intelligence one cannot say. *But now I knew that somehow, some day, all would be well.*

In July and August there were two further very clear and powerful dreams, not recorded here because they contain personal information about other individuals, that seemed to confirm my belief and again suggested the new university term as a significant time ahead. In this period, also, there were two similar and quite amazing events of deeply spiritual significance.

If nothing else so far has persuaded you that, however weak and faithless we may be at times, a sincere heart can receive answers to prayers, perhaps these will.

S   **30th July 2004: late at night, in the most beautiful part of my garden, I prayed for Bettina – that she might be healed of her pain – and acknowledged that I didn't have a clue what to do to help her or our situation. I put the problem in God's hands and lit a candle to represent faith. This candle was a small tea-light, in a rattan holder suspended by a thick nylon cord from a bird table; I had used these things many times before. But next morning I discovered that the cord was burned through and the holder had fallen to the ground.**

Not only has nothing like this ever happened before or since, I also have no idea how it could happen naturally since there was more than six inches between candle and cord – and these candles generate hardly any heat especially in the open air. I intuitively knew that this was an answer to my prayer: there would be a complete change in the situation, the difficulties 'cut through". And perhaps Bettina would in some sense 'fall'…

S   **23rd August 2004: about a month later I visited Westminster Abbey, one of the holiest places I know and a feature of an important dream in October 2003, and again I prayed for us. Then I went to meet a friend for lunch. But, because of some intuition, not only did I insist that we go to a different restaurant than the one my friend had planned, but having sat at a table outside I felt the need for us to change tables twice! (This was the same friend who had been with me when the computer printer jammed.) After a while, I began to describe my visit to the Abbey and just at this moment a large parasol just above us collapsed, grazing my head slightly and then smashing the glasses in front of us.**

We were the centre of attention in the street and the management offered their apologies, but I knew that this was an act of God! The answer to my prayer was the same as before: a sudden change, a fall, a failure of 'protection'...The critic may argue of course that, like the candle, this was 'just one of those things'. But why had I felt the need to change restaurants *and* tables so that we were in exactly that place?

When does a *coincidence* become a *synchronicity*? Surely the point is the meaningfulness of the event, whether it has a real importance in the mind and in the life of the experient, who in turn is the only one who can make that judgement. My friend John told me a wonderful example. He was feeling bored at work and wondering whether his football team's manager was going to be sacked after a run of bad results, but there'd been nothing on the news. He turned to a colleague, who supports a different local team, and began to discuss the matter. Immediately, the colleague's telephone rang and simultaneously John received an email on his computer – it was from a friend who told him that the manager had in fact just resigned. The colleague's call was from a different friend telling him the same news. Now, the event may have had a reasonable probability, but four independent individuals were involved in this exchange which all took place in a moment. It is a wonderful, amusing and interesting *coincidence* – but nothing *more* than that because the event had no great life significance for these individuals (though it might have done for the manager).

It may be argued that many of the events that I have described are little more than this: fairly interesting coincidences. "So what if the candle fell? That umbrella too would have fallen anyway..." "There are lots of cars with number plates that spell something..." (actually, there aren't). But I am noting these things and reporting them because of their *meaning* for *me* at those *moments*. This is synchronicity. And if it happens to you, only you can be the judge of it!

Similarly, just two days after the umbrella incident:

S   **25th August 2004: I saw three car plates in quick succession, first ... CLU then ... 03 DAN then ... BET. The** reference in the Book of Daniel is to "deliverance from the fire".

But I knew that the time wasn't yet quite right when a few days later I returned to work after the summer holiday to find that **the A41 roadworks *still* weren't finished!** Just one junction, a right turning, remained closed off... On the other hand:

S   **10th September 2004: on this road, in quick succession, I saw the cars ... BET and ... 923 JOB which refers to God "moving mountains".**

From this point the synchronicities really started to proliferate again, at an average rate of about one a day, virtually all of them encouraging. There were car references to a meeting, to healing, to miracles and to God responding to prayers. Again I found that I'd recorded some music in error, the song Trying To Reach You. Then there was another of those seminal dreams...

D   **23rd October 2004: A 'spiritual teacher' was standing near me and showed me a vision, rather like stars in the night sky joined by lines. I understood that each circle represented a significant situation in life, with many connections between them and to me (in the centre).**

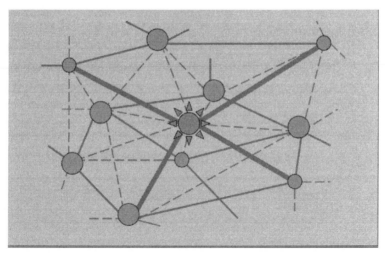

The being spoke to me: "In our lives we experience many situations and relationships. Some of these are vital for our growth, while others are just practice. But while we live, we cannot know which are which…So, in every moment, we must try to be the best that we can be."

As he spoke, parts of the web faded from view to leave only a few 'vital' centres and links visible.

This was so *lucid* that it was perhaps not so much a dream as a visit to another world. The words spoken were heard perfectly clearly. The being with me stood just behind and to one side, its presence entirely real. I woke up immediately afterwards, completely alert and with total recall of the experience.

It was the most powerful encouragement to me to go on believing in what is good, however hard life may be, and to know that we are supported and guided on this path.

About two weeks later, the long-awaited change was triggered by another of my 'ordinary' dreams!

D   4th November 2004: In my car I approached a major junction in my home town of Wolverhampton, but I was held up by a cyclist just in front of me. He was wearing sunglasses and listening to a Walkman through headphones, and was weaving slowly across the road, obviously unaware of anything around him. I got out of the car to remonstrate with him, pulling off the glasses and headphones. Then I saw that the road just ahead was being reconstructed – it was wide and straight and almost finished.

S   4th November 2004: The next morning I saw the car number … 655 JOB, which passage includes the words "God grant me what I long for".

The dream clearly speaks of a major turning point approaching and a new, clear path ahead. It's time for me to wake up, to look and listen! The follow-up sign also seemed to tell me that the time was now right – though I still wasn't at all sure how. Nonetheless, acting on instinct I went three days later to leave a note and a flower at Bettina's door. At the first road junction of this journey, **I was delayed by a man crossing the road wearing sunglasses and headphones, obviously unaware of where he was.**

Then, nearing her house, I saw **... 44 DAN which includes the words "How great are God's signs!"** The weekly horoscope spoke of **"...perhaps a surprising reunion...a chance to start afresh..."** During the next morning, I opened my office door and **a white feather blew in...**

Φ

Five days later, the telephone rang in the middle of the night. It was Bettina. She was in distress and needed to talk to me. It was the breakthrough, the 'fall', the turning upside-down. We talked throughout the night and then I went to her house to comfort her; the feeling between us was just the same as ever it had been.

She was still, rightly, cautious about our 'relationship' so things moved slowly but throughout the next several weeks we were in touch and growing inexorably closer. Naturally, I was impatient! But whenever my faith began to wobble again there would be signs and dreams to strengthen me. For example, one day when I felt very low and was wondering whether things really would work out, **I saw the familiar car M 106 ARK as I parked outside a laundrette.** This reference – "Be prepared..." – has always been reliable. An hour later, as I began to take my washing out of the drier, **I found lying on top of it an American quarter dollar coin. I have no idea how it got there; I had never seen one before let alone possessed one. I picked it up and read on it the words "In God we trust"**!

Then, as this extraordinary autumn term came to a close:

S   13th December 2004: **The A41 roadworks were finally finished and the new turning was open!**

S   15th December 2004: In my first Christmas cracker of the season I found a plastic ring…

S   25th December 2004: Bettina and I met for lunch on Christmas Day and it was a very, very happy time. As I set off to go home I saw 286 JON which describes Christ's first miracle, at a wedding.

D   27th December 2004: I was in unfamiliar countryside and nearing the end of a 'quest', holding a small coin and following written instructions about where to go. Some of the turnings and decisions that I had to make were very surprising, yet I obeyed the instructions faithfully and discovered that everything worked out perfectly, just as I'd hoped for. I finally arrived at a car where I met my lover. Then I saw a large number 55 appear in front of me.

Again I understood that I was being guided on this incredible spiritual journey and must simply trust in God (the coin in the dream echoing the one I had found recently) however difficult or strange the path. Some resolution and peace of mind was close – it was not too long until my 55th birthday!

The New Year was the happiest that I can ever remember, as Bettina and I spent it together.

IC   1st January 2005: My annual I Ching reading that day was Hexagram 37: "Family". The commentary describes a loving coming together, similar to my last birthday reading, resulting in "Grace".

A week later I read the book again, for the future of our relationship:

IC   7th January 2005: Hexagram 30 is "The Clinging, Fire". It describes the radiance of nature and the necessity of perseverance. The dedicated man must hold fast to what is right. Moreover, "that which is bright rises twice". The fourth, moving line speaks of a flaring up and a dying down, something being consumed too rapidly – this is what happened in our 'first relationship'. But the sixth line describes "The zenith of life. Good fortune comes from grief because of a real change of heart". This is our second rise. The resulting hexagram was 37, which I'd received the week before.

In the weeks that followed we grew closer than ever. This was a genuine renewal, for we were both different now as a result of the profound spiritual learning we were experiencing. But what hadn't changed at all was the deep bond that both of us had recognised right from the beginning. Life was not all plain sailing, but at this time it would have been very difficult not to believe in miracles. Just a couple of months before, joy seemed unimaginable.

I really hope that this offers strength and inspiration to others who may read this and who also suffer the terrible pain of the 'loss' of what they believe in and hope for.
Please never stop believing.

But life never stands still. We live in a world of constant change where the greatest spiritual challenge to each one of us is to discover that which never changes and to gain the strength to let go of our attachment to that which must pass. As many teachers have said before, when we are *attached* to other things (which are ephemeral) or other people (who are changing), then we stop growing. If our sense of personal identity *depends* upon that which is outside ourselves – be it a career, money, others' approval or even a relationship – then we lose touch with that which is within us, the true self. Such dependency inevitably makes us resist change, which is the natural state of life, and therein lies all our suffering.

This is what I had finally just begun to learn in 2004, when despite my loss I discovered that there remained an inner peace. I still felt the same deep love and it remained with me every day and in everything I thought or felt or did. I began, hesitantly, to realise that **this inner love does not depend upon any attachment to others**. Yes, I had discovered it through my relationships. It revealed itself more and in different ways with each blessed one of those of whom

I have written, and others. And ultimately it was Bettina whose great gift was to help me to break through my last resistance.

The love that I now felt no longer depended on our relationship or on everyday events. There were good times and there were still many difficult times. When times were good, this love could be expressed joyfully and powerfully, often with an almost transcendental sense of oneness. When times were bad, the love still felt just the same.

I had found the deepest sense of spiritual identity. **Awareness of this *is* love. This is the self. This is a consciousness of oneness, of the spirit. It is a capacity within oneself and so it neither depends upon nor belongs within any one particular relationship**. While it may seem, for many of us, to be focused on a special individual, it is just that our connection to that person *awakens* more deeply our sense of what is within us all. The world goes on changing, circumstances are never constant, and relationships may come and go. But this sense of love for and unity with all things and people is constant and timeless. (Perhaps those who do find this and share it with one special partner are the most fortunate people alive.)

I am quite certain that everyone we come to know has something to teach us, especially those whom we find most challenging. There are even some who believe that our souls make 'contracts' before birth, agreeing to teach each other certain lessons vital for our individual spiritual growth while living on the Earth. Personally I resist this thinking – too many tricky metaphysical implications – but nonetheless the purposefulness of my relationship with Bettina was clear.

Firstly, being 'in love' with her made every moment joyful and opened my heart and mind to that deeper spiritual love described. Secondly, the *difficulties* of the relationship challenged me over and over again to hold fast to what is true and eternal and to let go of any attachment to what really doesn't matter, to what is temporary. To return to an image from my first chapter, when one knows the river, its surface waves become less important. We may still be buffeted but the inner flow sustains us.

And there was a good deal of buffeting. This relationship was never easy. Her brave spirit had chosen the most difficult of paths in this life and she was carrying a lot of pain, with deep fears to overcome. Nor was I, to be sure, the easiest of characters to get on with. From the time of 'resurrection' in November 2004 we still didn't see each other frequently and she was still often holding back. These were the challenges to me. For all this talk of spirituality, heck, I'm still just a man and I wanted more – more of her, more of our happy times and, yes, more security. Godliness is all well and good, but there's nothing like the feeling of man and woman together…

She was changing, facing her own challenges, but life remained an emotional roller coaster. And even right from the beginning of this new ride, the signs and dreams began to tell me of further changes ahead. At the time, of course, I just didn't want to know. So may this be a warning: we must never drop our guard, never close our eyes to our awareness, always judge our guidance for what it is and not for what we want it to be!

The roadworks were finished. There was the Christmas cracker ring and the I Ching references to Family. These things and more convinced me that all would be well for us – the lasting happiness I longed for. After all, hadn't my guidance through all the terrible days been proved absolutely accurate?

But I forgot my own injunction that all things change. Indeed, within days of our coming together again, the warnings had begun.

D   **1ˢᵗ December 2004: I was sitting an exam in a room with several others. But there was a lot of unrest in the room which made it hard to follow the verbal instructions being given; I was angry that the situation was not being treated with respect. A certain question in the exam required me to match four people, named B, A, D and E, with some personal information given so that they would be happy. I found this very hard, especially for B, and felt under stress. Two women sitting nearby were being disruptive and provocative but the invigilators were taking no notice. Eventually I complained to the Chief Invigilator who at first told both the women and me to leave the room; but then she let me stay after all, and rebuked the other invigilators.**

This was clearly an anxiety dream! In recent years my personal challenge had been to find happiness with Eve, Dawn, Alice and now especially with Bettina, and life had often been unreasonably disruptive. Yet the dream suggested that ultimately 'someone' was being vigilant and things were under control. However, one week later…

D   8ᵗʰ December 2004: My father drove me and my pregnant wife to visit St Paul's cathedral. We had to walk the last part but she and I approached in different directions, mine involving a tricky journey around the edge of a lake. When I arrived, a big event was about to take place but I couldn't find my wife – the cathedral was crowded with people taking turns to sit down – and I was upset. Someone told me that it was important to be there at the end of the event because there would be music by Andrew Lloyd Webber. So I left, knowing that I had in my hand a special coin that would allow me entrance later, and retraced my difficult journey to the car.

Like Westminster Abbey before, the cathedral is a holy place that symbolised the spiritual goal to which we were being guided (dreaming of my father represents God for me) on our path; her pregnancy recalled a similar journey dream of just one year before, on 24ᵗʰ November 2004. The present dream predicted more difficult and lonely times, and my not being 'accepted'; I had to be very patient and trusting – the coin was clearly the American one found nine days earlier. Still, there seemed to be a reassurance that eventually I could find my place, and presumably ALW was some sort of clue as to when… This would prove true in an awful and quite unexpected way.

The clearest predictions of all appeared a couple of weeks later, ironically just as our renewed relationship became especially happy.

D   24ᵗʰ December 2004:
(1) It was the last day of the school year and I was discussing with others a certain teacher who was going to retire; it seems he had more than one home and for some reason this made me

feel betrayed. I hurried to my class after Break but found that I was free after all. However, in Period 6 there would be 'a penalty'.

I have noted before how intimations of bad times often occur during good times, and vice-versa, but I've never become any better at accepting it. One day later, Bettina and I would have one of our happiest times ever, and even that would be eclipsed a week later, but the dream clearly described the end of our relationship (the school year, retirement, break) in a period of 'six'. A second dream on the same night was even more unequivocal.

D   24th December 2004:
(2) I was with my lover at home preparing a meal of grains and vegetables, and then she went to get ready for something. I was left with all the work, on my knees, under stress... There wasn't enough food so I made more; I had to clear up some mess and do someone else's washing up; a washing machine I hadn't noticed before was coming to the end of its cycle. Den, a character from television's Eastenders, appeared and said, with a laconic shrug: "I must have got the timing wrong"! Then my lover came back in with someone else and told me she was going out, and it didn't matter because "We didn't have a definite arrangement." I felt crushed. The time was half past six.

This was truly shocking. Here was I, working hard on the tasks of spiritual nourishment and cleansing but apparently to no avail. The cycle would finally end, with my lover leaving me again; and as in the first dream of the night, there would be a sense of betrayal. I instinctively *knew* that '6.30' meant six months time (6 x 30 days), and that would be almost exactly ten ('Den'?!) years from the beginning of the journey this book describes. For a long time I had believed that it was an eight-year path but apparently I had "got the timing wrong". So midsummer of 2005 would after all be the most critical time. I wondered, too, whether I should now reinterpret the ring found in December as a reference to 'a closed cycle'...

The message was emphatically confirmed three nights later by further dreams.

D   27th December 2004: The first took place aboard a ship and ended with me wanting food but having to wait for the opening of a Club 18-30 (these numbers again representing the time 6.30). The second was described earlier on page 172, but what I omitted there was that at the end of my quest my lover was sitting in a Peugeot 306 car! The numbers 55 reinforced the prediction since my birthday was six months away. A third dream that night saw me at school at a New Year gathering with others, to be told that my relative Nell had died. I can only associate this with Thomas Gray's Elegy Written In A Country Churchyard: 'The curfew tolls the knell of parting day…'

So despite our present happiness, it seemed that there was to be another parting.

We were close again, she wanted to be with me and I was more than ever sure of my deep commitment. Yet the messages over the next few months were decidedly mixed.

S   31st December 2004: I gave a close friend a Fortune Cookie, chosen at random from a bag. The hidden message read: "A friend of yours will get engaged this year."

S   22nd February 2005: I saw the car 798 DAN, referring to God's wonderful power, just as I listened to a marriage proposal in a radio play.

S   10th March 2005: As I was thinking about our second anniversary the next day, I saw the registration TWO 1.

S   27th March 2005: At a restaurant for Bettina's birthday, we walked through several small rooms to choose a table (there were several vacant). When she eventually settled on one, we found a white feather, not at first visible, lying on it.

Several other registration numbers at this time referred to 'resurrection' and to 'miracles'. **There was even a... TRU followed by a ... JOY when we left a restaurant on Valentine's Day!** But were all these happy signs merely waking dreams reflecting my own inner desires and beliefs? Other dreams were giving warnings.

D **5ᵗʰ February 2005: I was a sailor on a ship in port, preparing for a voyage to start, knowing that at some point there would be a sudden signal to start. A couple of big waves came over us and I managed to keep a young woman safe, for which I received a commendation; I wore the letters 'I V' on my sleeve. Then I went to sleep, knowing that we would have to wake up and be ready to go in the middle of the night.**

Quite a few dreams at this time were featuring ships and imminent voyages while several car signs also related to Jesus 'entering a ship', further echoes of the November 2003 dream. The new journey was not far off (perhaps the letters I V could be read as Roman numerals, and four months from now would correspond with the other predictions). And while I wanted this journey to be with Bettina, I had to start facing up to a different possibility...

D **14ᵗʰ April 2005: I was living with Bettina but there was great tension between us. She complained that my radio was too loud; she was running a bath and the water was almost overflowing. Someone named Burns was about to come and take us to visit a hospice. I then drove into the countryside and across a bridge to a roundabout at a T-junction. I tried to go right but was feeling anxious and overshot the turn, coming to a stop facing another car going the other way and driven by a woman. So I turned left instead and found that my father was now driving. We were on a wooded hillside overlooking a broad river, where I saw a speedboat set off in our direction.**

Such tension was not evident when we were together, but I was clearly sensing it under the surface. Was I inadvertently putting her under pressure (the loud radio) and was the emotion we shared too much for us to handle (the bath water)? Was the relationship

214

going to 'flare up' and 'die'? It was deeply upsetting but mercifully the dream also offered some reassurance: through 'trying too hard' I might lose my way, but I would be guided on a new path (my father again driving) where things would progress rapidly (the speedboat). In the next few days, road signs reinforced this message. **M 106 ARK means "be prepared", then I nearly ran over a broken cycle, then M 406 ARK refers to the sower's seeds falling on stony ground while M 531 ARK mentions the 'breaking of ties'.**

Acting purely on instinct, as I had done twice before, I suddenly decided now to take my Reiki training a step further. I had never intended to become a Teacher, thinking it unnecessary, but now it seemed imperative; in my mind, it was going to be for Bettina's sake, to help ease her troubles. But in the back of my mind I remembered that the earlier levels of training had been at times when actually I had needed strength and guidance, ahead of the losses of Eve and of Alice... The first day of training was arranged for the end of May, which as it turned out was cutting things fine.

In the middle of that month, a close and dear relative of Bettina's died and she fell into a period of great sadness and anxiety. A week later she was at my house when an awful misunderstanding arose between us.

S   **21ˢᵗ May 2005: She left the house angrily and, in tears, I followed her into the road and asked her not to leave. At that very moment, the car M 886 ARK approached us. This is a reference to "...a sign". I knew immediately that this sign meant that she *would* leave.**

We made up, but in the next two days I saw:

S   **22ⁿᵈ May 2005: M 406 ARK again – the stony ground.**

S   **23ʳᵈ May 2005: S ... HOK followed by ... BET.**

During this week, I spent a few afternoons clearing her garden and planting flowers. Then I set about cleaning the paths and drive, the symbolism of which (for me) I have described before. But she arrived home tense again, there were more misunderstandings and then the worst argument we had ever had. Some air was certainly cleared, and new light shed on several things! We made up again, but…

S   **26th May 2005: … 137 ACT refers to the power of the Holy Spirit. Then in quick succession there were two different … ALY cars, which made me think of the initials AL(W) in the dream of 8th December 2004.**

S   **28th May 2005: M 404 ARK describes the sower thwarted again.**

S   **6th June 2005: I left a flower and a loving message at her house, but saw the car H … ELL.**

Next day she telephoned to end our relationship. I don't know why. It was the day of my students' **AL exam.**

Φ

I was in shock, and felt grief and pain for a considerable time, but I did not break down. For one thing, I had found inner reserves of calm and strength through the Reiki training. But more than this, even, somewhere in my mind I had known not only that this was going to happen but also that *it had to happen.* I could now begin to see that the 'mixed messages' of the last six months were not at all contradictory but indeed had all been accurate. On the one hand there had been so much joy; on the other hand, this parting and loss had come exactly as predicted, days before my birthday, marking the closure for me of a ten-year cycle of powerful relationships through which I had changed greatly. The wonderful continuation of the relationship had been as necessary as its ending. And now it was time to move on for, in the words of the I Ching a year before, all was gathered in.

Admittedly, I had wanted to believe that the cycle would end with a happier and more peaceful relationship, and of course my mind focused on Bettina. This was the intrusion of my own natural desires into the analysis of my spiritual guidance – after all, I am only human and merely a man at that. I had not anticipated several weeks of heartache and mourning.

But simultaneously I found that a very strange thing was happening: beneath the pain, at deeper levels of the mind, was a great peace and a completely unaffected sense of love. No anger. No blame. No *resistance* now. Just understanding, acceptance and love. I may have 'lost' Bettina but she, and all the others with whom I have been blessed to share this life, had given me the most precious of gifts.

IC   18th June 2005: Appropriately, my birthday reading was simply Hexagram 49, "Revolution".

And so a new journey began.

Nigel Peace

Appendix A: *The I Ching*

There are many methods of divination in widespread use, from the trivial to the deeply searching. It makes sense that we should try to learn from those who have gone before us and look at practices that have stood the test of time. Among the latter are astrology, rune stones and the tarot. What such approaches have in common is that, somehow, they enable us to access deeper unconscious levels of our minds where we come into contact with knowledge or understanding that is not clear to us in our normal conscious state. Our 'readings', therefore, are to be understood as *guidance* about the real or inner nature of a situation and perhaps also about how it might unfold in the future. We must also remember that our interpretations may be somewhat biased by our conscious thoughts, our expectations and our desires.

The I Ching, or Book of Changes, is one of the oldest known such methods, developed over many centuries in a philosophically very advanced culture. For readers who may be unfamiliar with it, this is the briefest of introductions intended only to reassure you that it is quite easy to use (although understanding its results may be more demanding!). There are many other good books describing its philosophy as well as many new translations; finding one that suits a particular individual is a matter of patient experiment. However, the version to which I have been referring is still widely regarded as the most faithful to the original, even if it does require an appreciation of metaphor and symbolism and an indulgence towards some of its more archaic language...

The importance of proper **preparation**, and the formation of a proper question, cannot be overstated. Use of the I Ching is not a party trick. If we are seeking to access the inner stream of consciousness, we are not likely to be successful if our attitude is superficial: "Right then, when shall I win the lottery?" This is not to say that money, for example, is not important; but the purpose of this kind of divination is to understand the underlying patterns, cycles and energies of our lives. So a more appropriate question might be "How can I improve my material security?" The I Ching 'responds' when it is approached with a particular issue, formulated in terms of our life changes.

If the question is too vague, so will the answer be; but on the other hand, if we are too specific we may fail to recognise that the book might be telling us something deeper and more important. If I ask the question "How will my relationship with so-and-so develop?" I might receive an answer that is clearly relevant to this relationship, especially if it is an important one, or I might read some more general advice about my approach to emotional relationships, especially if so-and-so is in fact not that important. It is an extraordinary quality of this book that it answers *the questions we should be asking* rather than, sometimes, the ones we do. So before even picking up the book it is worthwhile giving very careful thought to the question we are going to ask; equally, having put the book down, we should give careful thought to what question has actually been answered!

So clearly it is essential to develop a calm and thoughtful state of mind when consulting the book, in effect just as if one were about to address a spiritual guru. The responses often make one feel that this is exactly what has occurred. A mind in chaos or emotional turmoil, seeking an instant solution, is not going to be properly receptive to any good advice (Hexagram 4, by the way, is the book's way of telling the enquirer to go away and think about things more carefully!). So you should allow time for the consultation, at the very least thirty minutes, and ensure that you will not be disturbed. You will need pencil and paper to note the results as they occur. A sense of the occasion can be encouraged by some personal ritual, although this is a matter of individual preference. Personally, for example, I use candlelight and incense and focus my meditation on some religious objects that are meaningful for me, calming my thoughts and clarifying my question and its implications.

Φ

There are several **methods** used for carrying out the consultation. The most ancient and traditional one involves taking a bundle of 49 yarrow (or similar) sticks, then subdividing them in a certain way into piles and noting how many remain. This method has the advantage of being quite time-consuming and therefore in itself meditative – it helps one to focus on the process. However, I am not going to describe it here or even recommend it (any decent I Ching translation will give an explanation of it if you are interested), because on the one hand it is complicated and on the other hand I do not believe it gives fair results. The reasons for this will be given later.

Most people now adopt the 'coin oracle', which is easy to carry out (although some think its simplicity a disadvantage). Use three coins of the same type, perhaps Chinese, kept solely for this purpose: the tails or least decorated side is designated 'yin' (the feminine principle) and carries the numerical value 2, while the other side is designated 'yang' (masculine) and has the value 3. With the mind focused on your question, the coins are shaken between the hands and then cast together onto the table. The total of their values will be 6, 7, 8 or 9.

6 results from yin + yin + yin and represents a 'moving yin' line, drawn –**x**–. It is called 'moving' because it is entirely feminine and thus not in balance, so it must change.

7 results from yin + yin + yang in any order and represents a 'yang' line, ——. This is in balance and does not change.

8 results from yin + yang + yang in any order and represents a 'yin' line, – –.

9 results from yang + yang + yang and represents a 'moving yang' line, –**o**–.

You have now obtained the first, lowest, line of your reading; the procedure is repeated another five times to obtain a complete hexagram, or six-line figure, of which there are sixty-four possible (ignoring for the moment whether any lines are moving). There will be a page in your book telling you the number of your hexagram.

For example, you cast the coins six times and obtain 6, 7, 9, 8, 8, 7. Your hexagram is number 18:

```
    ——
    – –
    – –
    –o–
    ——
    –x–
```

There is a great deal to learn, if you are interested, about the procession of the hexagrams, their structure and inner meanings, but little of this is necessary to the actual reading. Each hexagram has a descriptive name and an introductory commentary describing the situation with which it is concerned; there is also a brief 'judgement' and, in most translations, an 'image' which describes the symbolism with which it is composed.

If you have not obtained any moving lines, the commentary is your answer: the situation is stable and the book's words advise how to think about it. Usually, however, you will have one or two moving lines and *it is the explanation of these that is the most significant part of your reading* since they address specific issues in the situation and describe how they might change. Make notes on everything you have read so far that you think might be relevant to you and consider what you are being told – often it is surprisingly direct and the text will always include advice about the spiritual, or 'superior', way to approach a situation.

When you feel ready to move on – and this might be several hours later – consult the new hexagram that results when your moving lines change their nature i.e. a moving yin line becomes a yang line, and vice-versa. The commentary (only) of this new hexagram describes the potential outcome of the situation you have asked about, given that you heed the advice in the first part of your reading. The above example would change to hexagram number 41:

```
 ———
 — —
 — —
 — —
 ———
 ———
```

It may be helpful now to review the reading described on page 20 as an example.

It seems to me that any method of consulting the oracle must be genuinely random if its apparently meaningful results are to be taken seriously. That is, there must be a theoretically equal chance of each possible result. If this is so then a reading that is clearly appropriate to one's question is all the more remarkable. Of course, some might argue that randomness doesn't matter because the mind is in any case somehow influencing the outcome, perhaps by some sort of telekinesis. But on the one hand we just don't know if this is so and on the other surely the mind will perform best on a level playing field.

When tossing coins there is an equal chance of heads and of tails. So the probability of a moving yin or of a moving yang line is $0.5 \times 0.5 \times 0.5 = 0.125$ or $1/8^{th}$. For a yin or yang line it's the same calculation except that there are three ways of obtaining each (e.g. yin + yin + yang, or yin + yang + yin, or yang + yin + yin) so the probabilities of these lines are each 0.375 or $3/8^{ths}$. Because these probabilities are equal, this method can be said to be genuinely random. We can also predict that on average one quarter of the lines obtained will be moving ones, which is a mean of 1.5 moving lines per hexagram. So it is normal to have one or two moving lines.

To check this, I reviewed sixty-four readings obtained over a period of just over four years. There was a total of 98 moving lines, an average of 1.53 per hexagram, almost exactly as expected. The numbers of moving yin and moving yang lines were, also as expected, nearly equal (47 and 51).

Moving lines per hexagram	0	1	2	3	4	5	6	
Frequency		10	27	18	3	4	2	0 (total 64)

(mean 1.53, standard deviation 1.19 unbiased)

From the point of view of statistics there is nothing very unusual in this distribution, showing that the method is fair. However, I also checked how many times each individual hexagram occurred, either as a first answer or as a result:

Number of occurrences	0	1	2	3	4	5	
Number of hexagrams	9	20	17	9	8	1	(total 64)

(mean 1.84, standard deviation 1.29 unbiased)

Of sixty-four readings, ten had no moving lines and the rest yielded a second hexagram as a result; thus one hundred and eighteen hexagrams were obtained altogether making the average just less than two per reading. If an I Ching reading were *simply a random exercise*, this second distribution should be evenly spread with more or less every hexagram represented roughly an equal number of times. But this is far from being the case. Indeed, nine hexagrams had never been obtained in this period while another nine had occurred four or more times. This suggests that the meaningfulness of the hexagrams is indeed a relevant factor in a reading, something that may be obvious to the devotee but needs to be pointed out to the sceptic. [6]

Now, an analysis of the probabilities involved in the yarrow stick method, by contrast, reveals some significant imbalances. While the expected number of moving lines is reasonable at 1.58 per hexagram, it turns out that a yin line is 1.6 times more likely to occur than a yang line and that a moving yang line is no less than 4.1 times more likely to occur than a moving yin line. [7] So this method is *not genuinely random*. Its results are likely to be biased in certain ways.

Finally, I offer a third alternative and simple method of consulting the I Ching that may appeal to some readers. It is genuinely random and produces a slightly lower mean of 1.42 moving lines per hexagram. Shuffle a standard pack of fifty-two cards and choose three without replacing them in the pack. Let a red card (diamond or heart) represent yin with a value 2 and a black card (club or spade) represent yang with a value 3. The total of the cards' values is 6, 7, 8 or 9 as before and this provides the first line of the reading. The cards are now replaced in the pack, which is thoroughly shuffled, and the procedure is repeated five more times.

Enjoy this incredible book!

---

[6] It would be very interesting to collate others' experience of these two distributions so that a meta-analysis may be undertaken.

[7] The mathematics behind these figures is rather complicated but can be provided on request.

Appendix B:
A Summary of the Dreams

One hundred and eight dreams have been described in this book, very many of which clearly show that it is possible to have foreknowledge of future developments and even of specific events. The time periods involved range from a few days to several years. These periods are shown in *italics* in this summary, to indicate just how extraordinary this phenomenon has been.

It is perfectly true that in many cases the full understanding of a dream was not possible until the events actually occurred, but this does not invalidate the assertion that there was a precognition. For example, often a dream would warn of particular upsets in a certain situation without an indication of when they would occur; nonetheless the subsequent events would be clearly recognisable as relating to the dream. Moreover the dreams often gave information that could not possibly have been known at the time by any normal means, perhaps concerning people who had not yet been met or the actions of others that even they had not yet considered.

However, the most significant observation to be made is that in more than one third of these dreams *a specific time period was indicated*, usually by means of numbers, and *was* understood at the time. These periods ranged from six days to six years. Dreams of this nature are marked by * in the summary.

Only the briefest description of the dreams is offered here but page numbers are given so that the reader may refer back to the details.

Φ

Nigel Peace

Page	Date	The dream
23	10.04.94	A detailed warning of specific events that occurred *7 weeks* later.
30	22.03.94	A warning of personal distress that developed during the next *1 year*.
31	22.01.95	A warning of personal upset over the next *6 months*, naming its cause.
31	18.08.94	A description of my life ahead over a period of *9 years* including the name of someone met *13 months* later.
32	30.08.94*	Precognition of events *1 year* and *6 years* ahead.
33	17.06.95*	Details of times and places concerning important relationships *3* and *5 years* ahead
35	16.11.95*	A physical description and timing concerning a relationship *4 ½ years* ahead.
38	06.08.96	Prediction of a relationship *4 years* ahead with the initial of a name.
39	08.08.96*	A second initial of this name and prediction of an event *630 days* ahead.
41	24.11.97*	Precognition of a significant date more than *2 ½ years* ahead.
42	27.01.98*	Another precognition of *2 ½ years* ahead.
42	24.04.98	A warning of personal upset *1 week* later.
46	10.06.98	Reassurance concerning a future relationship *2 years* away.
48	24.08.98	Further reassurance about this including a specific clue.
49	27.08.98*	Clues about time and place concerning this, *2 years* ahead.
50	19.09.98*	A suggestion of *4 year* time periods.
51	19.12.98*	Prediction of a relationship in *1 ½ years* time.

226

5P1R1T R3V3L4T1ON5

Page	Date	The dream
52	10.01.99*	A specific prediction of a meeting *10 days* later.
53	02 –04.99	Five dreams warning of personal upset that occurred about *4 months* later.
53	20.05.99	A warning concerning a named person.
54	25/28.5.99*	Two dreams suggesting *4 year* and *8 year* periods.
55	20.07.99	A dream of blessing (at the 4 year period).
57	11.08.99*	Apparent spirit contact with a named person, reassurance about relationships and suggesting a *4 year* period.
58	28.11.99*	Precognition of a relationship *6 months* ahead and of its ending *2 ½ years* ahead.
59	24.12.99*	Another prediction of this relationship in *5 months*, and a suggestion of two *4 year* periods.
59	01.00*	Four dreams predicting improvements, with specific clues, which occurred *5 months* later.
60	21.01.00	Another apparent spirit contact with a named individual.
61	09.03.00	Repetition of earlier information and precognition of *2 years* ahead.
63	05.06.00*	Another spirit contact predicting events over *2 months* ahead.
63	07.06.00*	A further suggestion of the *8 year* period and a specific name clue.
65	14.07.00	Concerning the spiritual nature of relationships.
66	25.07.00	A life review dream with spiritual reassurance.
68	27.07.00	A warning of loss but also a promise of recovery.
68	29.07.00	Prediction of personal and global events *14 months* later.

5P1R1T R3V3L4T1ON5

If you would like further information about the author's work, or would like to contribute your own experiences of dreams and synchronicities for possible future publication, please visit:

www.spiritrevelations.com